BEYOND A BINARY GOD

BEYOND
A
BINARY
GOD

A Theology for Trans* Allies

Tara K. Soughers

Church Publishing
NEW YORK

Church Publishing
19 East 34th Street
New York, NY 10016
www.churchpublishing.org

Cover design by Paul Soupiset
Typeset by Denise Hoff

Library of Congress Cataloging-in-Publication Data

A record of this book is available from the Library of Congress.

ISBN-13: 978-0-89869-005-7 (pbk.)
ISBN-13: 978-0-89869-022-4 (ebook)

Printed in the United States of America

Contents

Acknowledgments

As we are reminded in the book of Hebrews, we are surrounded by a great cloud of witnesses who allow us to run with perseverance the race that is set before us. When I finish a book, I greatly feel the presence of that cloud of witnesses, and never more, perhaps, than when I finished this book. Without the help and support of so many people, this book would not have been completed.

When I began to consider that perhaps I might be called to write the book that I kept hoping someone else would write, I contacted Sharon Pearson, an editor at Church Publishing and a colleague when I had worked in the Diocese of Connecticut. Her interest and enthusiasm shepherded it through the approval process at Church Publishing. I also want to thank Milton Brasher-Cunningham, whose editorial skills greatly improved this manuscript. I want to thank all those at Church Publishing who contributed to this book in so many ways.

I also have to thank those members of the trans* community and trans* allies who have shared experiences, ideas, and concerns with me. I have learned much in the writing of this book, both through direct contact and online contact across the world. I know how lucky most of us are to live in the United States, which, while it still has a way to go to be a place uniformly and openly respectful of the trans* community, is much more accepting than many other parts of our world. I would like to particularly acknowledge the Facebook group "Parents of Transgender Children." Although I discovered it too late for many of my initial struggles, I found it an invaluable source of insight, particularly for the issues that arise for children who can verbalize their gender identities at a young age. I would also like to thank the Rev. Gwen Fry, who helped me whenever I got confused by terminology or issues in the trans* community, and the Rev. Cameron Partridge, who read and gave invaluable comments on chapter one of this book. However, any mistakes are likely of my own devising.

Most of all, I thank my family. I thank both of my sons, who have been sources of great discovery throughout their lives, and whose lives and questions have challenged me and my understandings of God, allowing me to grow and to discover that God is bigger than I ever imagined. I also thank them for reading this manuscript and providing useful feedback. To my husband—reader, proofreader, and copy editor extraordinaire: I cannot imagine this book coming to fruition without your patient and painstaking efforts. I am truly blessed.

CHAPTER 1

In the Beginning . . .

Why This Book Was Written

It was October 2013, and I had just finished my PhD in Practical Theology, officially graduating on September 25. As part of our celebration of the official end of my doctoral program, my oldest child had planned to come home from college for the Columbus Day weekend. About a week before Columbus Day, we found out that work would prevent the trip home. We were disappointed at not being able to see our daughter, so my husband, my younger son, and I decided that we would visit instead. I emailed the news, but the email I got back was not what I expected. It had an attachment, labeled "letter, v.3." In the body of the email, our daughter said her dad and I should read the letter together. That is a statement guaranteed to raise the anxiety level of any parent. Fearful and concerned, I read it first, wanting to prepare myself for whatever we needed to deal with. I then went to get my husband, and I watched while he read it. Neither of us said anything. We didn't discuss the

letter—for us, there was really nothing to discuss. I sat down at
the computer and began to compose a response. It began with,
"We love you, we have always loved you, and we will always love
you, whether you are our son or our daughter." It ended with,
"Now call us—we need to talk about what all of this means."
When I finished, my husband (always the editor) made a few
changes in wording, and we sent it. Such was our formal beginning as parents of a trans* child—although we had actually
been the parents of a trans* child for almost twenty years, we
had had no idea before that email.

In many ways, our family was extraordinarily lucky. We had
a great deal of support. We lived in Massachusetts, one of the
most trans*-friendly places in the United States.[1] We were a part
of the Episcopal Church, one of the more open and welcoming
of the Christian denominations. Our background was privileged: while many of those who identify as trans* are people
of color, we were European American.[2] We had health insur-
ance that, while not covering all transition-related costs, was
required by the state of Massachusetts to cover some of them.
Our close family members were, for the most part, accepting
or at least neutral in their responses, and our church family
was very accepting as they watched the long-haired girl in
skirts become a young man with a beard.[3] The combination of
all of these factors meant our eldest child was spared some of

---

[1] I use the term trans* to describe the whole spectrum of genders that are covered
under that term. For a fuller description of terms, see the final section of this chapter.

[2] Analysis of data from the 2015 U.S. Transgender Survey, adjusted for the higher
response rate of whites to internet surveys, estimates the trans* community as 62.2
percent white, 16.6 percent Latinx, 12.6 percent black, 5.1 percent Asian, 2.5 percent
multiracial, 0.7 percent American Indian, and 0.4 percent Middle Eastern. National
Center for Transgender Equality, "The Report from the 2015 U.S Transgender Survey,"
Transequality.org, 52, accessed August 4, 2017, http://www.transequality.org/sites/
default/files/docs/usts/USTS%20Full%20Report%20-%20FINAL%201.6.17.pdf.

[3] While violence is very common against trans* people, those most at risk are trans*

the trauma common to trans* people in our society.[4] In addition, I had done a great deal of studying about gender issues, most recently in my PhD work. I had friends and associates who were gender-nonconforming. I knew more about gender issues than most people who had not dealt with them personally (with themselves or with a close friend or family member). I knew what some of the issues were likely to be, something about the path of transition, and perhaps all too much about the dangers of identifying as trans* in our culture.[5]

Being of an academic turn of mind, my first step was to immerse myself in anything I could find that would help me to understand my child's experience more deeply, so that I could be more supportive and a better advocate. While there is still relatively little theology written from a trans* perspective, more is being published all the time. Unfortunately, much of the earlier

---

women of color, especially black trans* women. They seem to suffer disproportionately from the prejudice and fear that come from violating societal gender norms, a toxic mix that is often labeled trans* misogyny (a hatred of trans* women). A good way of learning about the difficult experience of a black trans* woman, even in a culture that is reasonably open to trans* people, would be to read Janet Mock's memoir *Redefining Realness: My Path to Womanhood, Identity, Love & So Much More* (New York: Atria, 2014). A more theoretical approach to the scapegoating of femininity is provided by Julia Serano's *Whipping Girl: A Transsexual Woman on Sexism and the Scapegoating of Femininity*, 2nd ed. (Berkeley: Seal Press, 2016).

[4] In the year prior to the survey, 46 percent of the respondents were verbally harassed, 10 percent were sexually assaulted, and 9 percent were physically attacked because of their gender identity. People of color and other vulnerable populations suffer at the highest rates. National Center for Transgender Equality, "The Report from the 2015 U.S Transgender Survey: Executive Summary," Transequality.org, 4, accessed August 4, 2017, http://www.transequality.org/sites/default/files/docs/usts/Executive%20Summary%20-%20FINAL%201.6.17.pdf.

[5] The rate of violence is high in schools, causing 17 percent of trans* people to leave school early as a result. The rate of poverty for trans* people is far higher than the norm in this country. They are twice as likely to live in poverty if they are white and five times as likely if they are people of color. Among those trans* people who were gainfully employed, 30 percent had suffered mistreatment in their workplace due to their gender identity in the year before the survey. National Center for Transgender Equality, "Executive Summary," 3–4.

theological work assumed that trans* issues were simply a subset of general LGBT issues. Although gay and lesbian writers often included trans* people as a minor category, the issues are distinctly different.[6] While I think I would have had no issues with whomever my children were attracted to, it was quite a shock in some ways to discover that I had been mistaken about a critical part of my child's identity. Gender identity, at least for me, was more challenging than sexual orientation.

My first reaction was, "How could I have lived with him for so long without knowing who he really was? How could I have not known that he was male? How could I, who thought I knew him well, have been caught by surprise by his announcement?" Since gender is such an important category in our culture for identifying who people are, it took a while before I could accept that I knew many more important things about my son than his gender. But I was puzzled. Many books describing common trans* experiences talk about how early the sense of being wrongly identified can arise, often as young as three years of age. I had read stories about children insisting upon being addressed by their proper gender or refusing to wear the clothes of what they identify as the wrong gender. We had seen none of that. Our son never insisted that he was male until he came out when

---

[6] An early work that shows this characteristic is *Omnigender: A Trans-religious Approach*. Originally written in 2001, Virginia Ramey Mollenkott uses the term "transgender" as an umbrella term that includes all who deviate in any way from cultural norms of gender expression or presentation. She does not really use trans* in the same way it is used now, primarily to talk about gender identity. Virginia Ramey Mollenkott, *Omnigender: A Trans-religious Approach*, 2nd ed. (Cleveland: Pilgrim Press, 2007), 12. A more recent book that assumes that theological issues around transgender people can be neatly folded into the LGBTQIA spectrum is *Rainbow Theology* by Patrick S. Cheng. Cheng focuses upon constructing a "rainbow theology," by exploring the intersection of race and ethnicity with sexuality. Except for the Indigenous theologies that include the two-spirit people, Cheng barely mentions trans* people at all. Patrick S. Cheng, *Rainbow Theology: Bridging Race, Sexuality, and Spirit* (New York: Seabury Books, 2013).

he was nearly twenty. He had liked horses, as many girls do; he had a huge collection of plastic horses, and his stuffed animal collection was equally large. He was also into arts and crafts and music. On the other hand, he had not liked frilly clothes or the color pink as a child, but I hadn't thought much about it. After all, I don't like frilly clothes or the color pink either, and I did not consider that to be unfeminine. He liked outdoor activities, but many girls do. He was uncomfortable with the way his body changed during adolescence, but few adolescents are entirely comfortable with the process. All in all, I was rather proud that I was raising a girl who did not feel obliged to adhere to what I considered outdated gender conventions. I wanted my daughter, as I thought of him at the time, to be free to choose what to like and to wear, and I was proud of "her" individuality.

Perhaps I was blinded by what was in front of me. I suspect that if I had held more rigid gender roles, I might have seen these deviations from them differently. If my husband and I had been intent upon upholding traditional gender roles, we might have come more quickly to the realization of "what was wrong with him," which is how he expressed that feeling of discomfort in his own body—what is called dysphoria. As far as his father and I knew, nothing was actually wrong with him. From adolescence onward, however, he felt that there *was* something terribly wrong, but he wasn't sure what it was. Since he couldn't identify and express what he was feeling, he kept quiet and tried to fit in. The time of illumination came for him in his second year of college. When he went to a meeting of his college's 100 Percent Society (a society for everyone, no matter what gender orientation or identity), someone asked him what pronouns they should use for him. He recalled it was like being hit with a lightning bolt. He had never realized he could have a choice about the pronouns others used to describe him. Those words finally unlocked what was going on within him.

While I fully supported my son in claiming his own identity, I found myself grieving. I had enjoyed having a daughter, or at least the illusion of having a daughter. I felt a keen sense of loss. Although I much prefer reality, and I would much rather have a relationship with my real son than my illusory daughter, I did have to deal with my own grief. I also found myself feeling very guilty. Over and over again, I tried to figure out how I could not have known that my oldest child was a boy. Surely I should have seen that something was wrong. Surely I should have realized how much he was struggling. If only I had seen it earlier, I might have been able to support him better in his struggles. I felt a failure, not because my oldest child was trans*, but because I had not been able to support my son when he most needed support. I had not been able to help him to claim his true identity.

Most of all, I found myself confused by language issues. Although my son chose a new name similar to his previous one, making that transition relatively easy, changing the cursed pronouns was not nearly so simple. We use pronouns without thinking about them much; after almost twenty years of using one set, I did not find it easy to switch to another. At the beginning, it required a great deal of concentration. In fact, I found myself changing every female pronoun to a male one in order to try to get it "right," which left me identifying all kinds of women as "he." In some ways it was easier to do it right when my son was around, especially as he began to change physically. When he was away, however, it was far too easy to slip into old habits. Perhaps the hardest thing to change was using pronouns when I was talking about historical events. When my son was young, we had used female pronouns, and when I talked about an event in the past, those old pronouns came back to haunt me. For example, should I use male pronouns when I talk about what my son did in Girl Scouts? I eventually managed to do things such as excise the "Girl" from "Girl Scouts," but until I did, I kept tripping all over myself, getting stuck in the middle of stories I no longer knew how to complete without revealing things I did not feel comfortable revealing in casual conversations.

What was I to do with people who knew that I had two children who were ostensibly a girl and a boy? When should I explain, and when should I let it slide? When should I correct people who refer to my eldest as a girl or by his childhood name,[7] and when was it not worth it? How much should I say to people who were not close friends or family? For the story was really my son's story to tell, even though he usually left it for me to deal with when we were together and this issue came up. In a world and a culture fixated upon identifying people first and foremost by gender, how do you cope when your child does not easily fit society's understandings of what it means to be male or female?

Those were my early struggles. Although I can't say I have succeeded in banishing all of the issues that were raised in the first days of my son's transition, I have become a lot more comfortable talking about what has happened and explaining my family configuration to others. The number of books and other resources available to help families and other allies in this work has expanded dramatically in the last few years. There is a lot of advice on explaining gender identity to those who are curious and confused. There are resources about appropriate (and inappropriate) ways of responding to someone whose

---

[7] Among the trans* community, their previous name is often referred to as their "dead" name after transition.

gender is unclear or puzzling. Issues common to trans* people have become more visible, as gender-nonconforming people and their allies have worked to try to make our culture a safe and welcoming place for all people. While many of the trans* people I know think that Caitlyn Jenner was far from an ideal public model for trans* people, her very public coming out did increase the level of conversation about what it means to be trans*. Through lots of study, work, and talking with trans* people, I have come to a much deeper understanding of gender identity than I had when my son first told us that he was trans*.

As I worked through some of those initial struggles, however, theological issues began to raise their heads. Many trans* people are rejected by their religious communities, and often those who are rejected by their families are rejected on religious grounds.[8] Religion has been one of the strongest supports for traditional gender roles and gender norms, too often punishing those who dare to step outside of their prescribed identities and roles. Joan of Arc, who led the French armies to victory and was captured by the English, was eventually burned alive, not because of her role in war (for it was the French who eventually condemned her, not the English), but because she went back upon her promises, including the promise to wear women's clothes.[9] Although Pope Francis has been willing to be more compassionate toward gays and lesbians, in a recent question-and-answer session in Krakow, Poland, he described the teaching of children about transgenderism as ideological colonization and quoted Pope Benedict, who called gender transitioning a "sin against God

---

[8] About half of the trans* people who were surveyed and were out to their families experienced some type of family rejection, and more than one-third of those who had been part of a faith community left that community for fear of rejection. National Center for Transgender Equality, "Report," 75–77.

[9] Sven Stolpe, *The Maid of Orleans: The Life and Mysticism of Joan of Arc* (San Francisco: Ignatius Press, 2014).

the creator."[10] Although he publicly embraced a trans* man who asked if there was still a place for him in the church, Francis has stated that the teaching of gender theory (which he defines as the idea that one can change one's God-given gender) is like nuclear weapons: a step toward the destruction of God's creation.[11] While Francis believes that Jesus would not abandon trans* people and the church should provide pastoral care for them, he also believes that those who transition are committing a sin, just as are homosexual people who are not celibate.[12] For Pope Francis, and Roman Catholic theology in general, gender remains a strict binary, with each gender having a prescribed and complementary role. To challenge that binary is, therefore, to challenge God's design. Many other religious groups also believe that it is impossible to change one's gender in ways that do not correspond to one's biological sex. They see their role in the way that Pope Francis does: helping people to come to peace with their gender dysphoria. However, there are many Christians who have moved away from a strict binary understanding of gender, embracing an understanding that acknowledges that gender identity falls on a spectrum.

Unfortunately, the reluctance of many Christians to see the gender binary as cultural rather than God-given has made the lives of many trans* people very difficult. Many homeless

---

[10] The Vatican, "Dialogue of the Holy Father with the Bishops of Poland," July 27, 2016, http://press.vatican.va/content/salastampa/it/bollettino/pubblico/2016/08/02/0568/01265html.

[11] Joshua J. McElwee, "Francis Strongly Criticizes Gender Theory, Comparing It to Nuclear Arms," *National Catholic Reporter*, February 13, 2013, https://www.ncronline.org/news/vatican/francis-strongly-criticizes-gender-theory-comparing-it-nuclear-arms.

[12] Nicole Winfield, "Pope Francis Urges Pastoral Care for Transgender People, Draws Line between Ministry and 'Indoctrination,'" *Washington Post*, October 2, 2016, https://www.washingtonpost.com/news/acts-of-faith/wp/2016/10/02/pope-francis-urges-pastoral-care-for-gay-transgender-people-draws-line-between-ministry-and-indoctrination/?utm_term=.11824a563dea.

youth are LGBT (lesbian, gay, bisexual, or trans*), and have been thrown out of their homes due in part to these theological beliefs. According to the Williams Institute, 40 percent of homeless youth are LGBT.[13] Of these youth, a disproportionate number are trans*. Of those surveyed, about 40 percent of trans* people have attempted suicide in their lifetimes (a rate about nine times the national average)[14] and, as noted earlier, trans* people also have a much higher rate of unemployment. Even among those states that forbid job discrimination against those who are gay or lesbian, few have similar protections for those who are trans*. Too often, those who have little knowledge of the research around gender identity or acquaintance with trans* people think that trans* people don't really exist. Many religious leaders will claim, as Pope Francis does, that trans* people have been deluded by others who tell them that they can choose to be whatever gender they want to be. Few trans* people, however, think that gender identity is a choice. The choice they actually have is not in choosing what gender they are. Their choice is between whether to be honest about their gender identity or to hide in a cloak of societal respectability. As gays, lesbians, and bisexuals have also discovered, there is a cost in pretending to be who you are not. For trans* people, that cost is higher than for most. They are not merely hiding who they are attracted to; instead, they have to hide who they really are. That need to hide, or else face extreme prejudice and violence, makes the tragically high rate of suicide understandable.

I could—and did—affirm to my son that I believed that all people were made in God's image and likeness, and beloved by God. However, I realized that I had never really thought

---

[13] National Coalition for the Homeless, "LGBT Homelessness," National-homeless.org, accessed December 30, 2016, http://nationalhomeless.org/issues/lgbt/.
[14] National Center for Transgender Equality, "Executive Summary," 8.

through the issues the experiences of trans* people raise for traditional theology, and how the experiences of trans* people might broaden our theological understanding and enrich our understanding of God. As a practical theologian, I believe that our understanding of God is influenced by our context and our practices. How, then, is our understanding of theology different in a context in which there are people who do not fit the idea of traditional gender binaries? Even trans* people who identify as either male or female challenge the immutability of gender. Those identifying as non-binary challenge the very idea that gender is a duality. What does it mean to understand gender in a way that affirms that it cannot be contained within a simple two-gender system based upon the appearance of genitals or even chromosomal makeup? What does it mean to understand that the primary determinant of gender is not the nature and type of genitals but may be brain chemistry?

Early in the process, I searched desperately for resources that would help me to answer these questions, but few were available. Even now, several years later when more has been written in the area of trans* theology, what I was looking for—an in-depth discussion of theology for trans* allies—still does not exist. As the trans* community focuses upon issues of survival, which is a necessary first step, trans* theology is still very much in its infancy.[15]

Although I had initially hoped that someone else would do the work for me, I found myself feeling the need to help others through this minefield. As a parent of a trans* man and as a theologian, I could not avoid the theological questions. I needed to make sense of it for myself, if not for my son. Over the last

---

[15] One contribution in this area is Justin Tanis's *Trans-gendered: Theology, Ministry, and Communities of Faith* (Cleveland: Pilgrim Press, 2003).

several years, as I have seen the ways in which Christian theology has been used to oppress or even to deny the existence of trans* people, I knew that I did not have the luxury of remaining silent. So it was that I began to think about writing the book that I wished someone else had already written.

This is not a book of theology for trans* people. I cannot write from that perspective, not being trans* myself. Instead, I write out of the context of a trans* ally. Although theologians once believed that they could write theology from a totally "objective" point of view, the many varieties of liberation and contextual theologies have taught us that the "objective" point of view is almost always the view of the dominant members of a society or group. All theologians write from their own perspective, even if they attempt objectivity. As a practical theologian, I am very aware of how much context affects the way that we think about God. I need, therefore, to be honest about my own context.

I write theology from the perspective of someone who is white, cisgender (a non-trans* person), heterosexual, economically and academically privileged, the parent of both trans* and cis sons, and a priest in the Episcopal Church. My context means that my theology may not fully engage trans* people, who approach theology from a different set of experiences and contexts. Many who identify as trans* in the United States do not have the privileges that I experience. Because of the lack of support for gender-nonconforming people in our culture, some are homeless, and some are forced to work in the underground economy in order to survive. Because of the lack of family support and the difficulties associated not only with transphobia but also with racism in our culture, many have not had the opportunity to receive the type of education that I did. I cannot construct a theology from a trans* perspective, no matter how I try, for I have not shared in that experience.

What I can speak to is a theology that makes sense from my experience as a trans* ally, and offer it for trans* allies. I hope it will help allies to see trans* experiences not as something that destroys traditional theological norms, but that indeed breaks open our theology—which has often been bound by rigid understandings of gender—in new and exciting ways. When we can get to that point, we realize that trans* people do not represent disruptions of our community life, but are, instead, gifts from our gracious God that open us to new understandings—not only about human nature, but also about the nature of God, in whose image we are all made. Our challenge is to accept and to be thankful for the gifts our trans* members bring our communities—gifts that, like all of God's gifts, require us to grow in ways that may not be easy or comfortable.

This is the book that I wished had been available when I was struggling with theology in the context of learning to be a trans* ally. You have your own experiences that you bring to this work; this is my offering to those who take both trans* experience and theology seriously. In particular, I am interested in how the biblical view of humans as made in the image and likeness of God helps engage and broaden our understanding not only of what it means to be human, but what it reveals to us about God. After a short discussion of terminology, I invite you to explore these ideas with me, so that we who are allies can proclaim that all people are indeed made in the image and likeness of a God who is not binary.

Some Notes about Terminology—or, What the Heck Is LGBTQIA+?

There are few issues more confusing or more controversial than how we use language. For most groups that are in the minority, how they are named is an issue. It is those who have power in society who often assert the right to apply names—and while some groups may proudly take on the negative names and claim them as their own, most argue for the right to name themselves. This is certainly true for the trans* community, for whom identity and name are key to their self-understanding. The problem is that there are varieties of opinions within the trans* community about what terms should be used. In order to be clear about how I am using terms in this book, I have listed below my way of defining the terminology. Be aware, however, that as you read other books or talk to members of the trans* community, they may favor other ways of naming their own reality.

To begin with, all of the letters that are usually strung together—LGBTQIA+—are not describing the same type of thing. They all have something to do with sexuality or gender, but that is as far as the similarity goes. It is like having a list of spaghetti, broccoli, chocolate cake, and raspberries. They may all be types of food, but that is as far as the commonalties go. The assortment of letters has to do with biological sex, sexual attraction, and how persons perceive themselves, as well as how they present themselves to others. There may be some things in common, and the letters may overlap in some ways, but comparing and contrasting is difficult. Many people identify with more than one of the letters. To help our understanding, we can categorize the letters as biological sex, gender identity, gender expression, and sexual orientation.[16]

Biological sex is usually assigned at birth. It is determined, in large part, by the makeup of our chromosomes, and leads to a certain form of our genitals at birth, causing doctors to proclaim, "It's a girl," or "It's a boy," at that time. During adolescence, those who have been identified as clearly female will usually develop the secondary sexual characteristics of women, while those who were clearly identified as boys will develop the secondary sexual characteristics of men. Biological sex, in the trans* community, is also often described as the gender assigned at birth.

Not all babies, however, are easily identified as male or female at birth. For a small fraction of babies (one in 1,500 to 2,000 according to the Intersex Society of North America) the genitalia are not clearly defined, or the baby may have both male and female biological markers.[17] These children are known as intersex (the "I" in the list of letters).[18] Until recently, doctors routinely pressured parents to agree to surgery very early for these babies in order to clarify their gender, and advised parents to raise them as if they had been clearly defined at birth. Some people who were born intersex were never even told of their own

---

[16] For a visual representation of what I am explaining, search the internet for "Genderbread Person." This can be a helpful way of understanding the differences between categories.

[17] Intersex Society of North America, "How Common Is Intersex?" Isna.org, accessed July 27, 2017, http://www.isna.org/faq/frequency. Note that although the Intersex Society of North America fought against early surgeries for intersex babies, and actually tilted practice away from such early intervention, it paid a cost. In 2008, it folded into the Accord Alliance to continue its advocacy under a less contentious banner. Its website, however, is still available.

[18] Not all members of this community find the use of the noun "intersex" to be empowering. Some prefer to speak either of intersex conditions or of disorders of sexual development. Some members of the intersex community consider themselves to be part of the trans* community, while others do not. This is not surprising, as the intersex condition can be due to a number of different factors.

medical history. The choice of gender was not assigned by chromosome analysis, but by whichever way it was easier to make the genitals look unambiguous.[19] The surgeries were often extensive and would usually leave intersex people unable to reproduce. Doctors believed that an ambiguous biological sex was more harmful to children than these surgeries. This view was challenged strongly by groups such as the Intersex Society of North America. The early response of doctors to intersex children implicitly affirmed that they believed gender to be more about socialization than chromosomal makeup. Recommendations for the treatment of intersex children are slowly being changed.

Gender Identity. Unlike biological sex, gender is a social construct. While all societies recognize male and female genders, the behaviors and roles assigned to the two traditional genders vary by culture. Some societies recognize more than two genders. The role that these other genders play in their society and how well they are accepted vary by culture, but most cultures accept that people are not so easily explained by just two genders. Modern Western culture, however, seems particularly resistant to acknowledging this form of human variability.

Gender identity is the gender that the person knows oneself to be interiorly. Those whose self-understanding of gender is inconsistent with their biological sex or gender assigned at birth are known as transgender, the "T" in our list of letters. *Trans-* means "across," so transgender individuals are those whose gender is across from, or on another side of, the gender they were assigned at birth. Alternately, those whose self-understanding of gender is consistent with their biological sex are known as *cis-*gender—in other words, "on the same side."

---

[19] For technical reasons, many intersex individuals were assigned a female gender, and parents were warned to enforce traditionally feminine behavior upon them.

Some people do not identify with either masculine or feminine gender. Those people often identify as agender. Others identify with both masculine and feminine genders, and often consider themselves gender fluid. Collectively, those who do not have a singular gender identity are often called gender queer, a variation of "Q" in the above list of letters.[20] Non-binary trans* people are those who do not fit into the binary understandings of gender. They can present as masculine, feminine, or androgynous; sometimes they can present differently depending on the context. Often they prefer to use "they/them/theirs" as pronouns, or other non-gendered personal pronouns that are becoming more widely used.

In the trans* community, especially among trans* people of color, the terms "tranx" or "trans* folx" are sometimes used to refer to people without specifying a gender, something that can be difficult in the English language. "Trannie" is considered a derogatory term in the trans* community and should never be used. Note that, in some literature, "queer" is also used to refer to all those whose way of expressing their gender challenges traditional gender norms, covering the whole range of letters listed above.

Gender Expression. While often related to gender identity, gender expression is a separate category defining how a person expresses or "performs" gender. Cultures often have expectations about how men and women should dress, how they should talk, what work they should do, and how they should look. The

---

[20] The Q in our alphabet of letters stands for queer or questioning. Queer, originally a derogatory term for the LGBT community, has been reclaimed by the community as a source of pride. It is often used as an umbrella term for those whose gender identity, gender expression/presentation, or sexual orientation deviates from cultural norms. Gender queer individuals are those whose gender identity is "queered," i.e., they do not identify with the gender binary.

way that a person expresses gender at any particular time can
either be consistent with their gender assigned at birth or dis-
sonant. Prior to transitioning, many trans* people may have felt
a need to express gender in a way that was consistent with their
biological sex but at odds with their gender identity. After transitioning, many feel a relief in being able to express their gender in
a way that is consistent with their own self-identity. _Transsexual_
is often used in place of transgender in some of the older literature, and it is still preferred by certain members of the trans*
community. However, transgender is preferred by many trans*
people because, although they identify with a gender not consistent with their biological sex, not all will decide to make a
medical transition, something that is implied by the term "transsexual." Trans* people are named by their gender identity. In
other words, a trans* man is one whose biological sex at birth
was assigned female, but whose gender identity is male. Likewise,
a trans* woman is one whose gender identity is female. Like
the other categories, gender identity is also a continuum. Many
people, even those who identify as exclusively male or female,
show characteristics often associated with another gender. The
middle part of the continuum is often referred to as non-binary.
Those who identify as non-binary often express their gender in
ways that are neither exclusively male nor female.

There may be other people who express gender in ways that
are inconsistent with their own gender identity. Many cross-
dressers have no particular desire to claim a gender identity that
is inconsistent with their biological sex, but feel a need on occa-
sion to express themselves in a way that honors the part of their
own humanity that mirrors another gender. For these people,
their primary gender identity often remains consistent with
their biological sex, so they are not usually classified as trans*,
but their gender expression falls into two different modes.

Sexual Attraction/Orientation. The final category is based upon both who one *is* (gender identity) and who one is *attracted to* (sexual or gender orientation). Those who are attracted to people of the opposite gender are known as heterosexual, *hetero-* meaning "different." Those who are attracted to people of the same gender are known as homosexual, *homo-* meaning "same." Women who are attracted to other women are known as lesbians, the "L" in our string of letters; men who are attracted to men are known as gays, the "G" in the list. Those of either gender who are attracted to both men and women are known as bisexual (the "B"); those who are not sexually attracted to either are known as asexual, the letter "A" in the string.[21]

For trans* people, the designation of heterosexual or homosexual is based upon gender identity. So a trans* woman who is attracted to men would be considered heterosexual, while a trans* woman who is attracted to women would be considered homosexual or lesbian. A trans* woman attracted to both sexes would be bisexual. Likewise, a trans* man who is attracted to women would be heterosexual, a trans* man attracted to men would be homosexual or gay, and one who is attracted to both would be bisexual.

What, then, do we learn in this discussion of terminology? I think that the most obvious thing is that human beings are complicated. We often try to make things simple—either/or—but humans rarely fit so neatly into binary categories. In creating human nature, God seems to have delighted in complexity rather than simplicity. In our biological sex, in our identities, in

---

[21] Asexuality can also be thought of not as a single, easily defined category, but as a spectrum. For more information on the agender spectrum, see Dominique Mosbergen, "The Asexual Spectrum: Identities in the Ace Community," Infographic, *Huffington Post*, updated February 2, 2016, http://www.huffingtonpost.com/2013/06/19/asexual-spectrum_n_3428710.html.

our expression, and in our attractions, humans cannot be neatly divided into either/or, and we do damage when we try to make people fit into categories that do not really describe them.

Although modern American culture allows a certain amount of freedom in the expression of our gender identity, it still enforces many gender roles and gendered understandings. Men who stay at home taking care of children are seen as not quite manly. Women are expected to spend a great deal of time dealing with their appearance, trying to look forever young, forever thin, forever sexy. Certain jobs are seen as not quite suitable for women. We have yet to choose a woman president, although other countries throughout the world have done so. Women who are ambitious are considered less than womanly. Violence against women is more accepted in our society than other types of violence. Men are expected to be sports fanatics. Cultural gender roles are still pervasive, and one of the strongest forces upholding traditional gender roles has often been religion.

Christianity has often colluded with culture in punishing those who challenge traditional gender expressions and orientations. A large percentage of homeless youth are LGBTQ and were kicked out of their homes for violating gender norms; a significant percentage of those are trans*. Many Christians believe that gender identity is always consistent with biological sex, and that modern society is simply confusing young people by telling them that they can pick their gender. In that assessment, we are inflicting great harm upon the trans* community. It remains much harder to be trans* in our culture than to be cis. Many trans* people attempt suicide, and their rate of unemployment is staggering. Living a life as a trans* man or trans* woman is more difficult. They will experience more discrimination and quite possibly violence as well. Yet, for many trans* people, living a life that is authentic to their gender identity is worth it. It is not a frivolous decision, but one that often requires much in terms of persistence, financial outlay, and grief, for little gain other than the chance to live authentically.

For many trans* Christians, this chance to live authentically is the pearl of great price. Like the person in the parable (Matthew 13:45–46), they have proven themselves willing to give up everything to possess this one thing: the chance to live in accordance with their gender identity. Unfortunately, living authentically in our world often demands a high price. For trans* people, that price can include family relationships, jobs, and even housing. Discrimination against people simply because they are trans* is still legal in many parts of the United States.

As Christians, we do a great disservice to the trans* community if we make light of their passion for living into their God-given identities. I believe we need the trans* community represented in our churches, for their lives remind us about the complexity of human nature, a complexity that mirrors the nature of God, who, through creation, shows a delight in complexity. With them present within our communities, we more faithfully image the creation about which God proclaimed, "Behold, it is very good."[22]

---

[22] Gen. 1:31.

CHAPTER 2

The Need for a Theology for Trans* Allies

Imaging Christ

In spite of the fact that Jesus's physical description is found nowhere in the Bible, I knew exactly what he looked like when I was growing up. All of the pictures in my Sunday school materials, children's Bibles, and religious artwork showed a pretty similar picture. If I had been asked to describe Jesus, I would have described a tall, thin man, with pale skin and light brown eyes. His hair was medium brown, shoulder-length, and wavy, and his brown beard was short and neatly trimmed. I would have been indignant if Jesus had been described any other way. Everyone knew how he was supposed to look: a lot like the men around me (except for the beard and long hair), a lot like the men in my culture, a lot like someone who would not stand out from the inhabitants of the town in which I grew up, who happened to be one hundred percent white. Not everyone had that experience of Jesus growing up, but as a white girl in Indiana during the 1960s and early 1970s, I did. I also knew what he did not look like: he did not look like me. Jesus was definitely male. At that time, I had never heard of Gregory of Nazianzus or his arguments about Christ.

The early fourth century CE was a time of a lot of religious tumult, controversy, and questioning. How did Jesus, God the Father, and the Holy Spirit all relate to one another? Were they all God, and if so, what kind of relationship existed between them? How could we have three and still consider ourselves a monotheistic faith? In addition to these Trinitarian controversies there were also controversies about Jesus. How could Jesus be wholly God as well as wholly human when divinity and humanity seemed to be mutually exclusive? Apollinaris and his followers argued that Jesus's body was human but that his mind, or perhaps his soul, was divine—that kept the pieces from mixing. Gregory of Nazianzus, a bishop and theologian, however, argued against that solution in a series of letters, saying that in order for us to be saved, Jesus needed to be both wholly human and wholly God. In a letter titled *To Cleonius Against Apollinaris* (Epistle 101), Gregory said only that which Jesus took on or assumed could be saved or healed. Since all parts of human beings had been affected by sin, all parts needed to be saved. Therefore, Jesus needed to be fully and completely human.

> For that which he has not assumed he has not
> healed; but that which is united to his Godhead
> is also saved. If only half Adam fell, then that
> which Christ assumes and saves may be half
> also; but if the whole of his nature fell, it must
> be united to the whole nature of Him that was
> begotten, and so be saved as a whole. Let them
> not, then, begrudge us our complete salvation,
> or clothe the Savior only with bones and nerves
> and the portraiture of humanity.[1]

If the soul of Jesus was only divine and not human, our souls would not have been saved; if the intellect of Jesus was simply divine and not human, our minds would still be left in sin. Since the whole human was saved, Jesus must have been wholly human as well as divine. This understanding of the nature and role of Jesus made Christianity quite different from Judaism, its parent religion.

While early Christians and Jews were united in their repugnance for making idols or images of God, the question soon arose about representations of Jesus. The Decalogue forbid representations of God, as God could not be adequately represented by material things and images. If Jesus was fully human, as the early church councils had affirmed, however, could not Jesus be portrayed in artwork? The controversy over representations of Christ was an acrimonious one in the early centuries of Christianity. In general, the churches in the east were much more comfortable with images of Jesus than the western

---

[1] Edward R. Hardy, ed., *Christology of the Later Fathers* (Louisville, KY: Westminster John Knox Press, 2006), 218–19.

churches, and a great divide arose. In 787 CE at the Seventh Ecumenical Council, the controversy was finally settled in favor of those who wished to portray Jesus in artwork. The decision focused upon affirming that Jesus was indeed fully human, however, and not upon depicting Jesus in any particular way, which led to a flowering of Christian artwork. Since there were no early pictures of Jesus or any physical descriptions in the New Testament, the way that Jesus was portrayed varied, often taking on the characteristics of the communities and cultures that commissioned the artwork.

Jesus was and has continued to be portrayed in a variety of ways. Skin color, ethnic characteristics, clothing, and other markers vary notably in representations of Jesus—a fitting sequel to Gregory's theological understanding that in order for us to be redeemed by Jesus, he had to share in all of our humanity. The variations in the way Jesus has been portrayed tacitly accept that Jesus "assumed" all of these human forms, as all of these ways of being human have been "redeemed."

Many feminine images from the Bible, such as the Wisdom figure, Sophia, were used to describe Jesus in the early church, prior to the flowering of visual art—even Mother was a term applied to Jesus. However, by the time the controversy around artistic representations of Jesus was settled, Jesus was being portrayed as exclusively male, although sometimes as an androgynous-looking male. While race and other characteristics could vary from Jesus's earthly existence (as they almost certainly did in the case of images of Jesus that were part of my childhood), gender was more fixed and attempts to portray a feminine Jesus were more controversial. Artwork, while mirroring theology, also has the power to influence theology, and the portrayal of Jesus as only masculine left women a step further removed from

God than men were. Was womanhood also assumed by Jesus? If not, did that mean that women were not fully redeemed?

The issue of gender is also problematic if Jesus is to serve as a model for Christians. How can someone who is only seen as male serve as a model for women? Women were instead encouraged to see themselves as brides of Christ, or to model themselves after Jesus's mother, Mary. In the early Church, there were many women who served as leaders of Christian communities, but as the centuries went by and Christianity became an established religion, women's roles became more circumscribed. Although this trend began in the later writings of the New Testament, women's roles in the community became more and more limited in later centuries. By the time that I was growing up, little was left of the more feminine notions of Christ. Christ as Wisdom/Sophia or Christ as Mother was not something I was taught, or something that was a part of my tradition. I remember one Father's Day sermon that was all about how God was like a father—in other words, hard, punishing wrongdoing, and rule-oriented—and how God was not like a mother—in other words, soft, comforting, and nurturing. The sermon also says much about gender understandings of humans in that time and place, as well as gendered understandings of the nature of God.

In 1993, the first Re-Imagining Conference, an ecumenical conference exploring feminist theology, was denounced by those who saw in its use of the image of Sophia in worship not the early Christian image of Christ, but a foreign pagan goddess. (The great church Hagia Sophia in Istanbul is usually called St. Sophia's. However, it was not named after a nonexistent saint called Sophia, but after Holy Wisdom, or Christ.) Any divine representations that were imaged as female in that time were seen as necessarily pagan, ignoring the Wisdom strand in early

Christian writings. Christ might be represented in a variety of forms, and from a variety of cultures and ethnic backgrounds, but, for most mainline Christians, the one thing that Christ could never be was feminine.

Using Gregory of Nazianzus's understanding that what has not been assumed cannot be redeemed, what does that say to women about their salvation? If Christ does not encompass the feminine as well as the masculine, does that leave women unredeemed? A common solution, and one often quoted in the Bible Belt where I was raised, was to return to the biblical story of the Fall in Genesis and proclaim women are not redeemed by being like Christ, but by childbearing and submission to their husbands.[2] In a time when the subjugation of women was being questioned throughout our culture, this made it clear to many women that a gender-sensitive understanding of theology was necessary.

The Rise of Liberation and Contextual Theologies

Although the need for a gender-sensitive theology became more obvious to women and some men, many in that time (and some even today) resisted the notion that theology, which had been thought to be unchanging, needed any updating. While white males, and particularly white male academics, claimed that their theological understandings were universal—applicable to all and not context-dependent—few persecuted minority groups found much comfort in a form of theology in which their experiences were not taken into consideration and which

---

[2] Gen. 3:16.

often cooperated with culture to keep them in a subordinate role. However, from its beginnings, theology has been contextual. As Christianity spread across the globe, its evangelists found that they needed to retell the Christian story in ways that would make sense to new audiences and in new cultures. Many practices were incorporated into Christianity from other faith traditions, including the timing of many important Christian holidays, such as Christmas, Easter, and All Saints Day. For a faith that focused upon God becoming human, such enfleshing of the message of Jesus in new form might seem obvious, but it has often been highly controversial. Fears of losing the heart of the Christian message often made evangelists as much ambassadors for the norms of their culture as they were ambassadors for Christianity. Early English missionaries to Hawaii, for example, insisted that female converts dress in long woolen dresses like English matrons, attire not really suitable for the Hawaiian climate. Often practices that were a part of the culture were not only suppressed but demonized when missionaries came, alienating converts from their own cultural contexts.

Despite the attempts of missionaries to remake converts in their own image, however, the scriptures had a way of speaking to different groups in ways that their teachers may not have expected or even wished. Those who heard the message were often attracted to a different part than those proclaiming it wanted them to hear. But Jesus came, in his words, to bring good news to those who were oppressed, and in the gospel messages many who were oppressed have found their value in the sight of God, even if they were rejected by those in power in the world.

Owners of chattel slaves in the United States often justified their ownership with the idea that they were bringing Christianity, and therefore salvation, to their slaves. Early slave

owners were diligent in teaching Christianity, as it gave a veneer
of legitimacy to the evil practice of slavery. What they found
out, however, was that the slaves took to heart not the passages
in the Bible that entreated slaves to obey their masters, such as
Paul's justification for sending Onesimus back to his master
in the letter to Philemon (a favorite book of slave owners), but
the stories of liberation, particularly the freeing of the Israelites
from their slavery in Egypt, a story that was directly relevant
to their own life experiences. It was these stories that were
important to them, immortalized in their spirituals and the
images that fed them as they made their plans to escape to the
Promised Land. They empowered many enslaved people to resist
rather than submit to their fate, the exact opposite of what the
slave owners had hoped would happen. Alarmed, slave owners
began to regulate what passages of the Bible could be discussed
among the enslaved, because they had discovered that too much
Christianity could be a dangerous thing. The trouble was that
once stories had been learned by the enslaved community, they
were passed on through music and song, nourishing and sustaining a desire for freedom and a belief that God was on their
side. This effect on the oppressed has been seen time and time
again throughout Christian history.

In 1971 Gustavo Gutiérrez published *A Theology of Liberation*.[3]
Gutiérrez reclaimed the biblical message of Jesus as being one of
good news to the poor. He argued that Jesus stood with those who
were marginalized and oppressed, and he called for the Church
to join with the poor in opposition to those who oppressed them.
His call to challenge the social structures of the time, particularly in his native Peru, was highly controversial and was initially

---

[3] Gustavo Gutiérrez, *A Theology of Liberation: History, Politics, and Salvation*,
revised ed., trans. Caridad Inda and John Eagleson (Maryknoll, NY: Orbis Books,
1988).

condemned by the Roman Catholic Church. The fact that his social analysis used Marxist critique allowed many to dismiss it as a Communist plot. However, Gutiérrez's insight into the importance of Jesus's message to those on the margins of society ignited a movement that led to the development of many other theologies of liberation, theologies that come out of and speak to the experience of other oppressed groups.

In the time since the publication of *A Theology of Liberation*, many more branches of liberation theology have developed. Among the earliest successors were black theology and feminist theology. However, the idea that theology should speak to the experience of the people who are affected has led to a proliferation of theologies, all aimed at making the gospel relevant to the people of God in a variety of circumstances, all developing their own conversation about God (the word *theology* means words or conversation about God) in ways consistent with the gospel and their own experiences. Over time, we have seen great growth in our understandings of God as the diversity of experience leads to a diversity of conversations, which in turn leads us into a more expansive understanding of God and the way that God is at work in the world.

This expansion has not been uncontroversial, any more than other movements of diversity and inclusion in our society have been. It can seem very threatening to people who have been at home with earlier and less diverse understandings of God. Prior to World War II, many theologians believed that it would be possible to develop a completely consistent, rational theology. In that time period, grand systematic theologies flourished. The horror of World War II shattered the illusion in Europe that such a common, all-inclusive understanding was possible. The United States was more protected than Europe from the ravages of the war, and was slower to come to such an understanding, but rapid changes in demographics and the change in power relationships between groups within American society have led many theologians to talk not of developing one theology that is appropriate to all, but of developing theologies that are contextual and can speak to the diversity of people around us.

Not all Christians have accepted this notion, however, and often those areas that are most hotly debated focus around gender, gender identity, and gender roles. Within Christianity (at least after the Middle Ages), the notion of God ordaining two and only two genders, each with different roles in creation (what is often called gender complementarity), has been one of the most firmly held positions of those who decry the changing nature of theology and ethics.

Gender in the Christian Scriptures

In 2003, Dan Brown's novel *The Da Vinci Code* became a bestseller.[4] It is a gripping, fast-moving, well-written book, but I think the fascination with this novel went deeper than that. The fascination came from the premise that Jesus had a wife (Mary Magdalene), and that he had physical descendants who could be traced to present times. The thrill of the book was enhanced by Brown's painstaking research. He did not make up the story that Jesus was married. It actually has a long history, stretching back into the early Christian centuries, and there have been groups who have claimed such a lineage. That much is factually true. What is unproven is that there were actual blood descendants of Jesus. Even more unlikely is that they would have been

---

4 Dan Brown, *The Da Vinci Code* (2006; New York: Anchor Books, 2013).

able to secretly maintain the bloodline to the present. There is just enough factual material in *The Da Vinci Code* to give it the patina of a forbidden secret, and few things are more captivating in fiction than a secret that might just possibly be true.

Where did the story of Jesus being married come from? There is no mention of a wife (or children) in the New Testament, and you would think that would have been mentioned. Although Christians would later hold up the idea of celibacy as an exalted state, that was definitely not a Jewish ideal in the time of Jesus. A man in that time would have been married by age thirty. Since Jesus was a man, there must have been a wife around. Those looking for evidence of the wife he should have had searched the New Testament looking for clues. Jesus seemed close to a number of women, such as Mary and Martha of Bethany, but the woman who seemed closest to Jesus was Mary Magdalene. Early writings (deemed not worthy of inclusion in the New Testament) claim they had a very close relationship indeed, with Mary Magdalene being pushed aside in favor of Peter after the death of Jesus.[5] However, the more orthodox understanding was that Jesus, like the apostle Paul, defied the gender norms of the time and remained celibate, which was perhaps understandable because many of Jesus's words implied that the world would be ending shortly.[6] Certainly, when Paul encouraged people to remain celibate if possible, he did not believe that there was much time before the end of the world.[7] If the world was about to end, it made sense not to marry or produce families. In fact, if the end was going to be preceded by turbulent times, it would be better not to have young children who would

---

[5] One of those early church texts is the Gospel of Philip.

[6] See Mark 13:14–31.

[7] 1 Cor. 7:25–31.

be more vulnerable to such social unrest.[8] I doubt if Paul meant to enshrine the notion of celibacy in a church that would continue for at least two millennia after the time of Jesus. As a Jew, that would have been unthinkable. However, having heard from Paul that celibacy was a better state than marriage, what was the young church to do when Jesus did not return as quickly as they thought he would? By that point, celibacy had already attained a privileged position.

In 1988, an Episcopal bishop, the Rt. Rev. John Shelby Spong, shocked many Christians with his book *Living in Sin? A Bishop Rethinks Human Sexuality.*[9] Bishop Spong was a controversial interpreter of the faith, interested in how to make sense of the Bible in contemporary times. In his well-researched books, written for a broad audience, Spong tended to insert bombshells to ensure they would get a large amount of publicity. *Living in Sin?* was no exception. In the chapter in which he addressed biblical understandings of homosexuality, he speculated about why Paul remained single even though he, like Jesus, would have been raised in a faith and culture in which celibacy was not only unusual, but also highly problematic.

First, Spong analyzed Paul's pronouncements on homosexuality. Aside from quotations from the book of Leviticus in the Hebrew scriptures, almost all of the biblical comments on same-sex sexual practice are found in the Epistles. (Jesus had nothing to say about homosexuality in the Gospels.) In his commentary on the book of Romans, Spong argued that homosexuality was not seen as a sin by Paul, but rather as a consequence of the sin of idolatry. He pointed to Romans 1:20ff:

---

[8] Mark 13:17–20.

[9] John Shelby Spong, *Living in Sin? A Bishop Rethinks Human Sexuality* (San Francisco: Harper & Row, 1988).

His argument was that in the worship of idols instead of the creator the worshiping creature became distorted. Truth was exchanged for a lie, and natural relations were confused for unnatural. Homosexual activity was regarded by Paul as a punishment visited upon the idolators because of their unfaithfulness. . . . He was not suggesting that there was a natural norm that was broken by homosexuality, but rather that homosexuality was itself meted out to those who rejected the God of creation. . . . It was an unnatural act for a heterosexual person to engage in homosexual behavior, he argued. He did not or perhaps could not imagine a life in which the affections of a male might be naturally directed to another male.[10]

Spong further argued that since Paul's understanding about the genesis of homosexuality was not accurate on the basis of current scientific understandings, we needed to look elsewhere for an explanation of how Paul came to the conclusion that idolatry was at the root of homosexual activity. It would seem to me that it could be explained, at least in part, by the fact that same-sex activity between men, especially older men and younger boys, was practiced and accepted in the Roman culture of the time (and also that Jewish injunctions against it appear in the book of Leviticus). However, that is not the route that Spong took to explain Paul's association of homosexual activity with idolatry.

---

[10] Ibid., 149–50.

Instead, he delved into what we know of Paul's own biography. He never married and, according to Spong, "he seemed incapable of relating to women in general, except to derogate them."[11] Paul also spoke of himself as a great sinner, one unable to prevent himself from doing that very thing he did not want to do.[12] Finally, he talked of a thorn in the flesh that he had prayed God to remove, without success.[13] Spong noted these passages pointed to a man with a great deal of inner turmoil, centered in his view of himself. Although Spong did not assert that Paul was indeed homosexual in practice, he implied that Paul's thorn in the flesh could have been a homosexual inclination that made him view himself as negatively as he viewed those who engaged in the practice. Spong, referring to this thorn in the flesh, asked, "Was that connected with Paul's understanding of himself, of his own sexuality? If homosexuality could be viewed by Paul as God's punishment, could not whatever it was that ate at Paul's soul also be seen that way?"[14] In 1988, implying that Paul might be homosexual, even if a celibate homosexual, was explosive.

Both Brown and Spong pointed out that gender roles were more varied in the biblical tradition than many Christians had been led to believe—that both gender and gender roles were not fixed, unchangeable, and ordained by God. Neither of the two major characters in the Christian scriptures, Jesus and Paul, had fulfilled traditional gender roles associated with males, either in their time or in contemporary times, according to the biblical witness. In addition, Spong raised the possibility that Paul

---

[11] Ibid., 151. Although this point is highly debated, many of the Christian Testament passages used to uphold the subordination of women to men are found in the Pauline corpus, works either written by Paul or by his later followers.

[12] Rom. 7:15–24.

[13] 2 Cor. 12:7–9.

[14] Spong, 151.

did more than merely transgress gender roles, that perhaps his gender orientation was not heterosexual. The debates opened up by these books (and others that questioned traditional readings of the Bible around issues of gender and sexuality) have not yet been resolved in more traditional circles. The debate within Christianity around gender roles, gender orientation, and gender identity was just beginning in the 1970s and 1980s in many Christian communities. While new within the tradition to many Christians, however, this internal debate also reflected the debate that was swirling in Western culture. Even as Christians were beginning to engage with this kind of textual analysis of gender roles, "queer" studies were becoming more important in academia.

Queer Studies and the Rise of Queer Theology

Stephen D. Moore traces the flowering of queer studies to the annual meeting of the Modern Language Association in 1994 in San Diego. While women's studies and men's studies had been the foci of academic research prior to that point, at this particular conference queer studies, as a discipline, began to be imagined. Feminist studies and, later, masculinity studies had made the idea of gender—"the cultural product of a complex set of symbolic practices that mark (most) human subjects as either masculine or feminine"[15]—acceptable as a subject for academic study. In other words, for academic purposes, gender was seen as something that was not strictly biological, but had

---

[15] Stephen D. Moore, *God's Beauty Parlor and Other Queer Spaces in and around the Bible* (Stanford, CA: Stanford University Press, 2001), 13.

characteristics assigned by the cultural environment. Queer
studies focused more upon sex and sexuality. While gender and
biological sex are related but possible to distinguish, it is not
easy to cleanly separate gender and sexuality, as Moore points
out. He notes that Eve Kosofsky Sedgwick argued that "sexuality inhabits sex and gender simultaneously, deftly blurring the
boundary between them and causing each to lose its identity
in the other in a kind of epistemic ménage à trois."[16] Gender,
biological sex, and sexual expression, while not identical terms,
are related, each affecting how the other terms are understood.
For example, sexual expression between two people of the same
biological sex is often seen, in cultural terms, as quite distinct
from sexual expression between two people of different biological sexes—and not simply because of the way that the bodies
are involved; it is also framed in terms of the culture's understanding of gender and gender expression.

Despite Moore's claims that his own field, biblical scholarship,
is usually so far behind in the area of critical theoretical scholarship (theories about how texts should be studied and read) that
it often does not even begin to use a theory until after most textual scholars have abandoned it, he published a book on queer
biblical scholarship only seven years after that fateful MLA conference. His book, *God's Beauty Parlor and Other Queer Spaces
in and around the Bible,* investigated biblical texts for the places
in which gender, sex, and sexuality seemed to deviate from
norms of the time.[17] Those disciplines with the word "queer" in
their title seek to explore not what the culture identifies as the

---

[16] Ibid.

[17] Moore focuses on four places in his book: the shifting gender and gender roles
of the Song of Songs, the face and physique of Jesus in texts and art through the
centuries, the single apostle Paul's understanding of sexuality, and finally the book of
Revelation.

norm, but instead how what is defined as "other" is portrayed and how the "other" broadens the understanding of life within a time or culture. Moore argues that "queer" is a "supple cipher both for what *stands over against* the normal and the natural to oppose, and thereby define, them, and what *inheres within* the normal and the natural to subvert, and indeed pervert, them—this opposition and subversion privileging, but by no means being confined to, the mercurial sphere of the sexual."[18]

All cultures have preferred and "privileged" actions, classes, and groups. All cultures also have groups that, although present, do not have the privileges granted to other groups. This can be for a number of reasons. People have been discriminated against because of race, ethnic background, religion, and education, as well as biological sex and gender. While some cultures have been more open to ranges in gender, Western culture from early modern times (sixteenth century) into the present has generally insisted upon recognizing two and only two genders: male and female, of which one, male, is privileged. (In the Middle Ages, a third gender was considered common although not usually privileged; some cultures actually privilege those who do not display a strict gender binary.)[19] In modern Western society, biblical passages have been read with this cultural understanding of two genders, ordained by God, each with a set of unchanging gender characteristics. A quick look at history, though, demonstrates that gender characteristics have varied over time and been defined in different ways in different cultures—a sure sign that gender has a strong cultural component in its understanding.

The Western, strictly binary understanding of gender, sex,

---

[18] Ibid., 18.

[19] Christopher LeCluyse, "Performing Medieval Sexuality," H-Net: Humanities and Social Science Online, accessed August 7, 2017, http://www.h-net.org/reviews/showrev.php?id=25230.

and sexuality—often called heteronormativity—privileges male over female, female over any other gender, masculine biological sex over feminine biological sex, and heterosexual relationships over other forms of sexuality. This privileging is also endowed with the authority of religion. The Bible and other early church documents are typically read from that perspective, often blinding interpreters to other ways that these texts could also be read and understood. It sometimes requires additional work, however, to allow the Bible to engage in dialogue with modern ideas of gender, sex, and sexuality, for the books of the Bible were written across very different cultures and contexts. This lack of fit between modern understandings of gender and sexuality and ancient ones has opened up the possibility of finding, within the sacred texts themselves, affirmations of other forms of gender, sex, and sexuality. Using the tools of queer theory, Moore found many such queer spaces in and around the Bible, spaces that had been hidden or unexplored. He notes not only the lack of a wife for Jesus, but also that the way in which Jesus has been portrayed throughout human history has varied. As I said earlier, depictions of Jesus throughout Christian history have not been without controversy.

One of the most common images of Jesus from my upbringing was the *Head of Christ* painted by Warner Sallman in 1940.[20] This painting, which had such a formative influence upon me, did not show a "manly" Jesus, but a soft and comforting one, more in tune with Victorian pictures than with the rhetoric of the first half of the twentieth century that was determined to stress the "essential" differences between men and women, and make sure that Jesus personified the manly man. The *Head of Christ* was indeed disparaged by many evangelical teachers and

---

[20] The image can be found at www.sallmanart.org.

pastors of Sallman's time who preferred a more virile-looking Christ. Robert Paul Roth, a seminary professor, wrote a letter to the journal *Christianity Today*, in which he said that Sallman's *Head of Christ* was a "pretty picture of a woman with a curling beard who has just come from the beauty parlor with a Halo shampoo,"[21] demeaning the image for looking too feminine to truly represent Jesus. Although other artists of that time period painted pictures of Jesus as more traditionally masculine, Sallman's softer-looking, queerer Jesus went on to sell five hundred million copies worldwide. It was also this Jesus who provided an opening for less traditionally masculine-looking men to find themselves in Christ, and it was this portrayal, along with more androgynous images of Christ, that would lead those who had not looked traditionally masculine to believe that Christ could represent them as well. Moore details the transformation of Jesus from a traditional Palestinian Jew to this radiant hero figure, but a hero figure who was curiously soft.

When Moore analyzes the meaning behind the apostle Paul's single state, he reminds the reader that we need to be concerned not only about how other Jews might have interpreted Paul's celibacy, but also about the meaning that his single state would carry in a first-century Roman context. Although these two cultures have overlapping understandings, focusing upon the Jewish understandings is not sufficient, particularly for a figure like Paul who was a Roman citizen, educated in Roman ideas, and who was the chief evangelist to Gentile converts rather than Jewish ones. Roman society was strictly hierarchical, with the free (male) Roman citizen at its apex. Although homosexuality was common, men (*vir*) were defined as those who were dominant: those who were able to penetrate another and who

---

[21] Robert Paul Roth, "Christ and the Muses," *Christianity Today* 2 (March 3, 1958): 9.

were not penetrable.[22] Boy (*puer*), on the other hand, was the term used for male children, slaves of any age, and the passive partner in a sexual relationship. It was "inappropriate for a free-born male of sound reputation" to be the passive partner in a sexual relationship, for such a role rendered him not fully male, and such men were considered a horror. They had given up the manly dominant role for one that should be played only by boys, slaves, or outsiders.

Paul, celibate himself and recommending celibacy to others, would have been an abhorrent figure among Roman citizens, which may in part explain his lack of success among the upper-class Roman men. He did not assert his dominance and social status in the approved way by the penetration of others. In refusing to do so, he lost a great deal of social status, becoming a *puer* or an unman.[23] Instead of showing himself the dominant partner in his letters, Paul pictured himself as *puer* in relation to the dominant God who filled him. In Galatians, Paul proclaimed, "I have been crucified with Christ and it is no longer I who live, but it is Christ who lives in me."[24] Moore claims that the picture Paul's celibacy would have generated in the minds of the readers was that of the unman. "In this male-male love affair, Jesus is the penetrator, Paul the penetratee. Jesus is active and initiatory (cf. Gal. 1:12), Paul is passive and receptive."[25] In relation to Christ, he becomes a boy or an unman. Not only would this have been shocking to the Jewish readers of his time, it would also have been shocking to his Gentile readers. It is little wonder that many commentators focus not upon what Paul's celibacy would have communicated in his own time, but

---

22 Ibid., 139.

23 Ibid., 136.

24 Gal. 1:12.

25 Moore, 164.

on the reasonable theory that it was simply a concession for the end times. It would take queer scholars to point out what had been hidden all along. *reading into?*

From the insights of queer biblical scholars and theologians, the discipline of queer theology began to rise. Gay and lesbian theologians have been diligently working to challenge traditional understandings based upon accepted, but often not fully examined, texts. They have retrieved forgotten texts and found ones that had been hidden because their understandings were not always in accordance with modern ideas. This work has been invaluable in helping LGBT Christians reclaim their place in the Christian community, as well as in expanding the understanding all Christians have of the many ways that God has been and continues to be at work in God's people. They have raised important issues about the way that we interpret scriptures and have challenged our often overly rigid reliance upon a gender binary.

Their work has implications for trans* Christians as well. Such works of theology, by themselves, however, are not sufficient to make sense of the experience of trans* Christians. The resistance that many Christians have to the idea of flexible gender identity is far greater than to the idea of a variety of sexual orientations. In addition, gay and lesbians are now much more accepted culturally, and many more churches are open to their presence, but trans* Christians have not yet gained that level of acceptance, either in society or in Christian communities. Although most works of queer theology include trans* people, often their distinctive issues and questions are not a part of the discussion, and frequently their presence is only remarked upon in a couple of pages of these books.

The issues raised by sexual orientation are not the same ones that are raised by gender identity, and, ultimately, trans* theologians will need to develop their own distinctive way of talking about their experiences and understanding of God. What does it mean, theologically, to feel oneself to be a gender that is not the gender that your culture has designated for you? As an ally, and not a member of the trans* community, I am working on this theology secondhand. I am not attempting to craft a "trans* theology." That would be presumptuous: I cannot do that from the outside looking in. What I hope to do is offer some thoughts about how a theology that includes the unique experiences, challenges, and gifts of trans* people might look, but most importantly how we might begin this conversation in our communities. As many trans* persons have encountered destructive theological ideas that deny their identity, I also want to give some guidance for other trans* allies about how they might speak theologically about a loving God who wants all persons to live into their full potential. I will probably get many things wrong, but I hope that this book will encourage a wider conversation about how God is at work among all of us.

CHAPTER 3

Made in the Image and Likeness of God

Changing Bodies

While I was studying for my PhD, I took some classes at Boston College. A friend of mine, who was a graduate student there but also worked with undergraduates, told me something I initially found very shocking.

"What do you think is the most popular graduation gift for undergraduates at Boston College?" she asked. I tried a few guesses, but I was stunned when she said that it was plastic surgery. Surely she had to be wrong.

I have never been able to confirm her claim, but what I found out in looking for confirmation is that plastic surgery is becoming much more popular; in fact, many trendy magazines advocate the gift of plastic surgery to young adults, so that they can be their best, and feel confident and pleased with their bodies. In 2005, ABC News reported on the trend of giving plastic surgery as a graduation gift (in this case high school graduation), particularly to girls.[1] When asked why she did it, one mother answered, "This is a gift of love from us, and we see a difference in her."[2] When asked about the $7,000 price tag, she responded, "But I don't think you can really put a price on your child's happiness."[3] Another mother explained that she really wanted to give their daughter a car, but the daughter preferred breast implants, and she wanted her daughter to be happy. "I think she looks fine the way she is, but it's not my choice and . . . if it makes her happy, I'm happy for her."[4]

Whether or not it is as popular as portrayed in the press, plastic surgery—once the solution for bodies that had been disfigured or had not developed normally—has now become a form of medical intervention less concerned with restoring functionality and more intent on allowing people to approach cultural ideals of beauty. The most cited reasons for having the surgery are to make the young adult happier and more confident. The American Society of Plastic Surgeons reported that in 2015 there were "15.9 million surgical and minimally-invasive cosmetic procedures performed in the United States."[5] They

---

[1] John Stossel, "Why Are Parents Buying Their Girls the Gift of Surgery?" *ABC News*, July 16, 2007, http://abcnews.go.com/2020/story?id=875821.

[2] Ibid.

[3] Ibid.

[4] Ibid.

[5] American Society of Plastic Surgeons, "2015 Plastic Surgery Statistics Report," Plasticsurgery.org, accessed August 8, 2017, https://www.plasticsurgery.org/documents/News/Statistics/2015/plastic-surgery-statistics-full-report-2015.pdf.

reported the fastest-growing procedure was buttocks implants, a trend that the *Washington Post* claimed allowed people to have buttocks more like those of the popular media figure Jennifer Lopez,[6] demonstrating that even surgical procedures are influenced by the latest fads. Obviously, there has been a growing societal acceptance of people's right to reshape their bodies in ways that are important to them, which makes many people's rejection of gender reassignment surgery all the more puzzling. If a young woman can have breast implants to be happier or more confident, and a young man can have his breasts reduced in size to avoid embarrassment, then why the resistance to "top" surgeries among the trans* population? It cannot be simply that people believe that certain parts of the body should not be operated on. In the cases I mentioned, all are modifying the same part of the body. Yet, while people often view favorably the sort of elective plastic surgeries that make young women have larger breasts and young men have smaller breasts, the same is not true of surgeries designed to help one's physical body conform more closely to one's gender identity, if that gender identity is not consistent with the gender assigned at birth. The horror of the latter seems to be based not so much upon the idea of surgery to affect one's secondary sexual characteristics, but specifically upon the rejection of societal ideals of beauty based upon one's assigned gender. Women are allowed to have surgery to fit the cultural ideal of womanhood more closely, but woe to those who refuse to conform to traditional gender ideals. Linda Tatro Herzer points out the differences in the cultural response to surgery for cis and for trans* people:

---

[6] Ariana Eunjung Cha, "Plastic Surgery Is Surging in America—the Trends in Six Simple Charts," *Washington Post*, March 2, 2016, https://www.washingtonpost.com/news/to-your-health/wp/2016/03/01/the-surge-in-butt-implants-in-america-and-other-plastic-surgery-trends-in-5-simple-charts/?utm_term=.108a09d1c29d.

> And while it is okay for a cisgender (a person
> whose gender identity *does* match the gender
> they were assigned at birth) woman to have
> breast implants to align her internal image of
> herself with her external presentation, many
> people say it is wrong for a trans* woman to do
> exactly the same thing. . . . Personally, I think
> it is very important that we carefully consider,
> since we have no objections to people altering
> their bodies surgically or chemically for the
> sake of physical or mental health, why it is that
> so many object when the reason people want to
> alter their bodies has to do with gender?[7]

I believe that the root of these contrasting responses is the
belief that there are only two genders and that these genders are
able to be distinguished on the basis of physical sexual organs.
Although this has been proven to be untrue scientifically, as in
the case of intersex people,[8] the larger culture remains adamantly
binary in its understanding of gender, and often of gender roles
as well. That understanding has been bolstered by a particular
reading of the creation story in the first chapter of Genesis that
has been interpreted in ways that reinforce the understanding
that God created only two genders (male and female), that each
person was created one or the other, and that to question one's
gender was in essence to rebel against the God-given order of

---

[7] Linda Tatro Herzer, *The Bible and the Transgender Experience: How Scripture Supports Gender Variance* (Cleveland: Pilgrim Press, 2016), 61.

[8] For one of the first people to argue for gender as a cultural construct instead of a biological fact, using the presence of intersex people, see Judith Butler, *Gender Trouble: Feminism and the Subversion of Identity* (New York: Routledge, 2006), 127–44.

creation. As Herzer notes, this understanding "means it would be sinful to express oneself in a gender queer manner, as androgynous, bigender, or two-spirit[9] or as a cross-dresser."[10] In addition, the idea that men and women together are made in the image and likeness of God has led to the doctrine of complementarity, the belief that men and women are distinct, complementing each other not only physically but in the roles that they are called to perform. Christianity has done much to reinforce the binaries of gender identity and gender roles, and it continues to play that part, particularly in more conservative Christian traditions, for whom gender roles are at the heart of their understanding of what it means to be people of God.

I will argue that the passages that have been used to reinforce binary thinking often have more to do with cultural ideals than with theology and faith, and that there are other ways of understanding these scriptural passages that support the idea that all people are made in God's image and likeness, that all are beloved children of God, and that our culture's inability to recognize trans* people as fully human is a sign of the human inability to be fully open to the very real diversity that is a part of God's creation. In doing this, I am starting my constructive work on a theology for trans* allies.

---

[9] Two-spirit does not really fit in this list, as it has positive cultural connotations in Native American cultures and religions, although many in the Christian community would consider it sinful.

[10] Herzer, 50.

What Does It Mean to Be
a Theology for Trans* Allies?

In chapter one, I talked a little about what it means to write a theology for trans* allies. I acknowledged that, as a cisgender person, I cannot write a true trans* theology. I have not encountered the world through the experience of living as a trans* person. I have not seen through the eyes of the trans* community. I cannot decide how trans* people should understand theology in light of their own experiences. An important point of any theology of liberation is that theology cannot be completely generalized, but must be understood through the concrete experiences of communities. The theology I can work to develop is one that makes sense to me, and that might be helpful for other trans* allies: those of us who love and want to support trans* people who are often demonized, not only in the culture, but in our houses of worship as well. I am developing a theology to counteract the hate that so many trans* people experience, particularly in places where they should experience love and acceptance: their families and churches.

As I struggle to do this, I am aware that there is an underlying assumption to my attempts to speak of a theology for trans* allies, something that has come not just from my reading of scripture and study of theology, but from my experience as well. Since this belief is a debated point, I feel compelled to be clear about the underlying assumption that grounds my work, so that I am honest about what gives it meaning. I believe that trans* people, like all people, are part of God's creation, which means, for me, *a theology for trans* allies is a theology that takes seriously the fact that trans* people are part of God's creation, sharing in the goodness that all creation shares. While trans* people may sin and not live up to God's calling for them—as do*

all people—being trans* or transitioning is not a sinful act, but
one that is done to claim their God-given identity.[11]

My theology is likely to raise objections not only from those
who believe that there are two and only two absolutely distinct
genders; it also challenges those gender theorists who believe that
gender is completely a social construct, and for whom gender is
not an identity but a performance. In her book *My New Gender
Workbook*, Kate Bornstein argues that gender identity is not a
stable concept, because we change how we "perform" or express
gender in different contexts. According to Bornstein, when we
do that we are, in essence, changing our gender identity.

> I think it's a fact that identities, being false,
> require other identities to validate them—and
> that includes but isn't limited to gender iden-
> tity. Some people's gender expressions trigger us
> into changing our own. Here's how that works.
> When we shift our gender expression to accom-
> modate the gender expression of another, we've
> essentially shed an identity and put another in
> its place.[12]

I agree that gender roles and gender expression are heavily
influenced by culture, including interactions with those around
us. However, I do not believe that this shifting of gender

---

[11] As Herzer notes, "there are other Christians who see the physical realities of intersex conditions and the cognitive/psychological realities of the transgender experience as evidence of the Fall." Herzer, 57. In defining my trans* theology the way that I do, I am arguing against this understanding.

[12] Kate Bornstein, *My New Gender Workbook*, 2nd ed. (New York: Routledge, 2013), 114.

expression has to imply constant change in one's gender identity. Like an actor on stage, we may take on other ways of expressing ourselves (or communicating, in Bornstein's words) without losing our core identity.

There is more to gender than simply the way we decide to perform; in other words, gender is larger than our gender expression at a particular moment in time. Those whose gender identity is fluid may easily shift gender expressions in different situations, but, for many of us, gender identity seems to be more of a given and not simply how we decide to act at any particular moment. There is no doubt that much of the way we express our gender is driven by societal expectations and gender roles, but there seems to be more to it. The fact that living authentically and expressing their true gender identity is so important to many trans* people seems to point to an underlying gender identity that needs to be expressed, rather than a performance that creates a gender. I also suspect that some of the difficulty that cis people have in understanding the trans* experience comes from not having had to wrestle with that part of their own identity. While I often struggled with societal gender roles as a child growing up in Indiana in the 1970s, it was the expected performance of femininity that I found difficult, not my identity. Even as I wished for the very real advantages that males had in that time and place (and still do), I never wanted to be a boy. I wanted to be a girl who was not restricted by gender roles.

In the television series *I Am Cait*, Caitlyn Jenner reveled in her ability to do all of the girl-type things that she had not been able to do while living as a man. While certainly there are many trans* people who wholeheartedly embrace the cultural norms of masculinity and femininity, that is not always the case. There may be more pressure on them to follow those roles, especially as they try to blend in with cis members of their gender, but there are also trans* people who don't feel a need or a desire to engage in some of the performative aspects of gender expression. Gender identity and gender expression are not the same and do not necessarily even overlap (if that is confusing, you may want to review the differences explained in chapter one).

I believe authentic gender expression, while not determined by gender identity, flows out of the core identity of the person, one aspect of which is their gender identity. Although it may sound odd to those of us used to thinking in binary terms, a close look at God's creation shows that gender identity and gender expression are complex among all of God's creatures. While we may assume that the primary care of young is always associated with females, that is not the case with the spotted sandpiper. After mating and laying eggs, the female sandpiper flies off to find another mate, leaving the eggs in the care of the male. Not only does the male incubate the eggs, but he stays with the young birds for at least four weeks after they hatch. While we assume that gender is stable, that is not the case with the hawkfish. All hawkfish are born female, but if there are not enough males in a harem, then one or more of the females in the harem will become male and the harem will be split. If a male hawkfish loses part of his harem and then is challenged by a larger male, rather than fighting, as is the case with many animal species, the smaller male will revert back to being a female. While we assume that giving birth is associated with females, in sea horses it is the male that gives birth. There is great variety and complexity throughout God's creation, not only with human beings but with the animal population as well, indicating, just perhaps, that God does not always think the same way that we do about gender. In fact, perhaps the whole idea of binaries—either/or categories—is not something God created, but something human beings created to make the world a more comprehensible place. The trouble with making things more comprehensible, however, is that in doing so, we often ignore people or things that do not fit into our preconceived ideas.

Part of Original Creation or Fallen Creation?

The variations in both the natural world and humanity point to diversity as a core concept within creation. However, there are those who would argue that only the traditional male/female binary and heterosexual relationships are part of that original creation that God declared good. Anything else that exists is only a part of the fallen creation. Anything other than the ideal, in that view, shows the signs of sinfulness and is subject to God's judgment. Many Christians are quick to see God's hand in judgment after a catastrophe. Members of the Westboro Baptist Church have become notorious for their seeing God's judgment in all kinds of areas, usually in response to human deviation from what they consider to be God-given sexual and gender roles. They proclaimed that 9/11 was caused by America's increasing acceptance of gays and lesbians, and they even felt compelled to protest at the funerals of military personnel whose deaths they saw as due to our country's sinfulness. While most Christians find such theology appalling, the idea of a punishing God is still strong within our culture and within our Christian communities.

Such a theology does have biblical precedent. Before they crossed the Jordan River into the Promised Land, Moses told the people of Israel that they had a choice to make. They could choose life and length of days if they followed the Lord. However, if they allowed themselves to be seduced by the religion of the inhabitants of the land, they would suffer or even die.[13] Earlier in the Bible, we have God wiping out most of the population of the Earth in a flood because of their sinfulness.[14] Even earlier, Adam and Eve are kicked out of paradise because of their disobedience.[15] The idea that all that befalls humanity is due to God's system of rewards and punishments is indeed a strong strand in the Bible.

But there is a counter-strand in the biblical tradition. The book of Job is an extended argument against the idea that suffering means we are sinful. Job's "friends" echoed the theology of the day, insisting that Job must have sinned, because no one could have had such a succession of tragedies unless God were punishing him.[16] Job, however, refused to accept their analysis of his life,[17] and even demanded that God answer his charge that he was suffering unjustly.[18] While not really answering Job's question, God did seem more annoyed with the friends for trying to defend God's ways than with Job for challenging them.[19] The idea that suffering was a punishment for sin was so strong in Jesus's time that when the disciples encountered a man born blind, they asked Jesus, "Who sinned, this man or his parents, that he was born blind?"[20] I have always wondered how they thought someone could have sinned before they were

---

[13] Deut. 11:26–32.
[14] Gen. 6:17–20.
[15] Gen. 3:14–24.
[16] Job 36:1–12.
[17] Job 31:1–40.
[18] Job 31:3–8.
[19] Job 42:7–9.
[20] John 9:1–3.

born, but nevertheless, they were sure that someone had to have sinned for this tragedy to occur. Jesus firmly replied, "Neither," asserting that sometimes what humans consider to be a tragedy can be a different way to glorify God.

Most Christians believe that, sometimes, bad things happen to good people, but when tragedy strikes, people often wonder what they might have done to deserve this punishment. In Elie Wiesel's book *Night*, he talked about how the Jews in a concentration camp in World War II struggled to find God in the midst of the horror of the camp. After being forced to watch the death by hanging of a young boy, one man asks, "'For God's sake, where is God?' And from within me, I heard a voice answer, 'Where He is? This is where—hanging here from the gallows. . . .'"[21] In the midst of what they were experiencing, God was not to be found in those punishing them without cause, but in the faces of those suffering the worst that could be inflicted on humans by other humans. Although suffering was often seen as a sign of God's disfavor, Wiesel refused to believe that. For Wiesel, the undeserved suffering that Jews experienced in the Holocaust was proof that suffering could no longer be considered as a sign of God's disfavor.

Most of us see disease and disability as tragedies, but what if, as hard as some of these conditions are, we were to see them not as deviations from God's good creation, but as integral parts of it? Many parents of children with Down's syndrome talk about how these children bring special gifts to their families. Those who have disabilities often assert that seeing them as missing something ignores their different and important abilities. Cobi Sewell, a deaf vlogger, talks about why cochlear implants are controversial in the deaf community. He argues that the deaf and hearing

---

[21] Elie Wiesel, *Night*, trans. Marion Wiesel (New York: Hill and Wang, 2006), 65.

worlds are just different worlds, one focused on hearing and one on sight; who is to say which is better and which is worse?

> The hearing people are born in their world. Just as we deaf are born in ours. We are who we are. There is nothing wrong with any of us. We are all okay. It's all about respect and perspectives.[22]

Perhaps the real issue is not so much that people have a diversity of types and abilities, but the ways in which our cultures place value on those differences, seeing anything that does not match the culture's ideal as being deficient. What if there is some larger purpose in this diversity, a purpose that we are in danger of missing in our quest for an ideal uniformity among people? What gifts are we missing due to our inability to really see the ways God is present in those bodies that do not match our culturally generated ideals?

Nancy Eiesland was a theologian who wrote from her experience of disability. She talked about an epiphany or manifestation of God she received that bore little resemblance to the God she was expecting to encounter.

> I saw God in a sip-puff wheelchair, that is, the chair used mostly by quadriplegics enabling them to maneuver by blowing and sucking on a straw-like device. Not an omnipotent, self-sufficient God, but neither a pitiable, suffering

---

[22] Cobi Sewell, "What I Think about Cochlear Implants," YouTube video, August 22, 2016, https://www.youtube.com/watch?v=VPt9mGxnL20.

servant. In this moment, I beheld God as a survivor, unpitying and forthright. I recognized the
incarnate Christ in the image of those judged
"not feasible," "unemployable," with "question-
able quality of life." Here was God for me.[23]

Far too often, we see God as the embodiment of the cultural
ideals of humanity, more specifically of men. The God that we
"picture" has a perfect body, full of health, vigor, and strength.
It is an image of power, and we imagine that we are made in the
image of God to the extent that we match this cultural ideal of
embodiment. Yet, as Eiesland reminds us, the early Church wor-
shipped a disabled God, one with punctured hands and feet, and
with a large wound in the side. The resurrected body of Christ
was a body still marked by human sin and suffering.[24] It was a
body far from being perfect. In this image of the disabled God,
we see a God who is intimately acquainted with human limita-
tion and suffering, one who can be marked as a survivor. It is
an image of God who "embodies the ability to see clearly the
complexity and the 'mixed blessing' of life and bodies, without
living in despair."[25]

Unlike the perfect God body that excludes people as a consequence of its perfection, the disabled body is one radically open
to the whole of human bodily experience. No longer are we made
in the image of God to the extent that we are perfect, but we are
assured that we image God even in those aspects our society
may label as broken or disordered. It allows not just those who

---

[23] Nancy L. Eiesland, *The Disabled God: Toward a Liberatory Theology of Disability*
(Nashville: Abingdon Press, 1994), 89.
[24] Ibid., 99.
[25] Ibid., 102.

fit a narrow definition of humanity to be seen to image God. Indeed, all of us in our less-than-perfect bodies may actually image God more fully than the more static and perfect pictures of God we have been accustomed to encountering. The image of a disabled God is an image of hope for all of us, whether disabled or temporarily able-bodied.

Made in the Image and Likeness of God

The Hebrew Bible, which Christians often call the Old Testament, is strong in its denunciation of the worship of idols. Although many of the surrounding cultures made physical representations of their gods, the Israelites were forbidden to do so. They were clear that their God could not be captured in the image of any created thing, even a human being.[26] So what does it mean to be made in the image and likeness of God, the *imago Dei*? Whatever it means, it doesn't mean that God looks like a human being.

Instead of a single image of God in the Hebrew Bible, we are given a range of metaphors to describe God. As feminist Christian theologian Sallie McFague notes, in addition to images that evoke human characteristics or roles, "We find—both in scripture and in our tradition—naturalistic, impersonal images balancing the relational, personal ones: God as rock, fortress, running stream, power, sun, thunder, First Cause, and so on."[27] This broadening of images of God is an attempt to

---

[26] Exod. 20:4–6.

[27] Sallie McFague, *Metaphorical Theology: Models of God in Religious Language* (Philadelphia: Fortress Press, 1982), 20.

prevent idolatry, the worship of something other than the God who cannot be imaged by people or things. It serves to remind us that when we use metaphors, as we are forced to do in reference to God, we acknowledge that metaphors point not only to what is similar but also to what is dissimilar. A metaphor is not the same thing as the original object. When we talk of a child as a "chip off the old block," we mean that they have some obvious similarities with a parent. However, the chip is not the same as the block, and, even more important, parents are not rocks from which children are chipped. Metaphors serve the purpose of helping us to understand something about the relationship between the two things being compared, not to reduce those objects to the metaphors themselves. When we talk about God as Father, one of the most commonly used metaphors in the Christian tradition (at least in our day), we have to acknowledge that, though we are attributing certain fatherly characteristics to God, God is not literally our father. We were not begotten by God having intercourse with our mother (unlike some Greek myths). God did not go to work every day to earn a living for God's family. God did not come to our sporting events, or dance recitals, or graduations, or at least God did not sit with the family in his best suit and tie on hard metal chairs.

Any metaphor can bring up both positive and negative associations. For those whose relationships with their fathers were not good, the metaphor of God as father can interfere with the possibility of developing their relationship with God. Those who had abusive fathers or absent fathers may want to invoke one of the many other metaphors for the relationship between God and human beings. That is the gift and the grace of having a God who cannot be pictured in a graven image or any one image. It allows us to see how our metaphors of God point to both what God is like and what God is not like. God can be pictured as father or as fortress, sharing some characteristics of each, but utterly different than either. McFague insists "that a piling up of images is essential, both to avoid idolatry and to attempt to express the richness and variety of the divine-human relationship."[28] Although we might prefer to leave the possible images of God radically open—one day we can appreciate the warmth and light of a fire, and another day we focus upon living water that cools our throat and gives us life—we are also forced to deal with the question of how human beings reveal the image and likeness of God, which takes us to the first biblical creation story (at least, the first one presented in the Bible), found in Genesis 1:26–28. It is an important passage, both for exploring what it means to be created in the image and likeness of God and because it is one of the biblical passages often used to deny the created reality of trans* people.[29]

Imago Dei and Genesis 1:26-28

Then God said, "Let us make humankind in our image, according to our likeness; and let them have dominion over the fish of the sea, and over the birds of the air, and over the cattle, and over all the wild animals of the earth, and over every creeping thing that creeps upon the earth." So God created humankind in his image, in the image of God he created them; male and female he created them. God blessed them, and God said to them, "Be fruitful and multiply, and fill

[28] Ibid.
[29] Herzer, 50.

the earth and subdue it; and have dominion
over the fish of the sea and over the birds of the
air and over every living thing that moves upon
the earth." (Genesis 1:26–28)

As I mentioned earlier, this passage is often quoted by those
who believe that one's gender orientation has to match one's
anatomy. God created them male and female, and there is no
mention of those who do not nicely fit into those two separate
categories. It is also one of the primary passages used to argue
for traditional gender roles for men and women: if both men
and women are created in the image and likeness of God, then
men and women bring different things to the understanding of
God's image and likeness. Therefore, men and women should
both be honored, but neither is free to transgress their God-
given roles. If they do, they are sinning. This position is held
by many conservative religious groups among the Abrahamic
traditions where questioning either the stability of gender or the
necessity of rigid gender roles and expressions is not allowed. At
the heart of the debate is what it means to be made both gendered and in the image of God.

Logically, those who most strongly argue for the complementarity of gender roles should be most open to the idea of God
encompassing both male and female attributes. However, these
are the very groups that fight most often against inclusive language and using metaphors for God that are not heavily masculine because indicating that men and women both are made
in the image and likeness of God gives women an equality and
an importance rarely found in these communities, or, frankly,
in many places around the world. Men by themselves, however,
do not fully image God, and therefore the use of only masculine

images and pronouns necessarily shows an incomplete or a distorted image of God.

How is it that men and women—assuming that the two genders together image God better than each by itself—reveal the image of God? The question implies there are some distinguishable characteristics that each gender brings to our picture of God that are missing without their contribution. It asks us to look at how men and women are different. Most arguments about difference focus on either physical characteristics or roles.

Let us look at physical characteristics first. When a child is born, those attending the birth will look at the external genitalia to determine if the child is a boy or girl. As someone enters into puberty, other secondary sexual characteristics cue people as to gender. The distribution of hair or fat, prominence of the Adam's apple, and pitch of the voice will vary due to the influences of estrogen and testosterone. For some people, these characteristics mark a gender that is fixed and unchangeable.

One problem is not everyone is born with clearly male or female genitalia. Those who are intersex may have sexual organs from both, or they may simply have ambiguous organs. During puberty, under the influence of the increased sexual hormones they may actually develop in a way that is surprising to those who thought that they had identified their gender at birth.[30] In more ambiguous cases, babies will often have operations to make their genitalia conform more closely to gender norms, leaving them frequently sterile and occasionally insensate during intercourse. Until recently, most doctors would convince parents

---

[30] Herzer says that the four groups of intersex people—46, XX; 46, XY; true gonadal intersex; and complex or undetermined intersex disorders of sexual development— account for approximately 1:100 births resulting in people being born intersex. Herzer, 54–57. That is higher than many estimates, but Herzer is using the broadest definition of intersex.

such surgery was the best course for the child, and parents would be instructed to force the child to conform to the chosen gender norms. It was believed that the environment could override the child's natural gender identification. (This, of course, is inconsistent with the idea that genitalia are definitive in gender identity.) Unfortunately, many children were harmed in the process. Some felt a need to transition back to another gender later in life or to reclaim their identity as intersex. Once the largest organization of intersex people, The Intersex Society of North America worked to halt the practice of "fixing" a child's gender shortly after birth.[31]

Those who are still attached to the idea of binary genders, when they are confronted with this type of genital diversity, will often fall back upon chromosomal evidence to maintain a biological basis for a fixed gender. They will say that all people with two X chromosomes are female and all people with one X and one Y chromosome are male. That, however, is also a problematic basis, because not all people have one of those constellations of chromosomes. How do you assign gender to someone who does not have the traditional chromosomal pattern for males or females? What does that make someone who has one X chromosome and no second sex chromosome, or someone who has one X chromosome and two Y chromosomes, or any of the other natural variations in human chromosomal makeup? Moreover, none of this makes sense in the context of the story in which the point is that humans are made in the image and likeness of God. Unless we assume that God has a biological body similar

---

[31] Archived information about The Intersex Society of North America can be found at their website, www.isna.org. Although they accomplished many of their goals, they raised the ire of many medical groups for their critique of protocols for intersex infants. In an effort to allow more effective lobbying, in 2008 ISNA folded their group into the Accord Alliance, a group of health professionals and advocates that they founded.

to human beings, with different possible types of genitals and chromosomal arrangements, then what do any of these have to do with our being made in the image and likeness of God? Gender is mentioned, but it seems not to be connected with physical sexual differentiations, at least in the case of God in whose image we are made. Perhaps it is not biological sex that is referred to in this passage, but gender—a gender that does not depend upon sexual differentiation. *Maybe not physical at all!*

I would also argue that if we cannot easily differentiate gender by sex, then culturally defined gender roles are similarly problematic in this passage. There are no standard culturally determined gender roles that have stood the test of time. In our time, when people talk about the traditional family, they are often discussing a way of distributing roles based on gender that arose in response to the Industrial Revolution. While there was a culturally approved segregation of work in earlier eras, the differences were often not so rigidly enforced as they were later. The whole family joined together to do the work that needed to be done and all genders and ages were involved in the work, as families did not live in a nuclear configuration, with parents and children living apart from their extended family network. Families stayed together, and generations often occupied the same home. Instead of work being separate from the home, the preindustrial societies' home was the place where work occurred, so it was easier for everyone to be involved in all facets of labor.

With the rise of the industrial age, work became separated from the home; both gender and age played an increasing role in determining expectations for the type of work family members would do. Men started leaving homesteads to go to their places of work and women were left in charge of the work in the home, a pattern that became enshrined as the "traditional" family. Because of this change, there was less flexibility possible for those whose skills, talents, or inclinations led them to roles outside of the newly strengthened gender roles. As the role of the home as a place of commerce decreased, women's sphere of influence diminished, leaving them only the affairs of the increasingly smaller homestead, until, by the 1950s, many women were restricted to those roles that were deemed private rather than public: the cleaning of the house, the feeding and raising of children, and eventually, the sustaining (although not leading) of Christian churches in the United States. Even today, when many people claim women have achieved equality, the majority of home tasks are still performed by women.[32]

As with the biological sex markers, the idea that we somehow image God by performing certain gender roles seems anachronistic, as God does not leave the family to make money to bring back to support them, or spend time cleaning homes and cooking food for the family to eat. How do these gender roles, then, support the idea that it is in our differentiated genders that we are made in the image and likeness of God? Some would argue the complementarity of gender roles is primary, showing a God who is mighty and powerful in the wider world, and also a God who is tender and interested in tending to our individual needs. If that is true, why do those roles need to be assigned by chromosomal makeup or genitalia? There are people with penises who are every bit as loving and nurturing as those with vaginas, and there are those with vaginas who are strong and commanding presences in the world. That complementarity could still be present even if roles and gender

---

[32] Bryce Covert, "Why It Matters that Women Do Most of the Housework," The Nation Online, April 20, 2014, https://www.thenation.com/article/why-it-matters-women-do-most-housework/.

were not connected with biology. Perhaps whatever Genesis 1:26–28 is trying to convey is not about making sure everyone is upholding their assigned gender. Maybe this passage is not about biology at all.

Interpreting the Concept of *Imago Dei* in Biblical Creation Stories

Challenges to Traditional Interpretations of Genesis 1:26–28

The first chapter of Genesis is a long, poetic description of the creation of all things. It does not read like a science textbook, but more like philosophy, theology, or even literature. On the first day, God created light and darkness, but day and night were not created until later; sun, moon, and stars are not the source of light. The sky was the dome that separated the waters below from the waters above, and rain was that water that escaped from the waters above to join the waters below. Most of us do not use this description of creation to learn all about the cosmos. Even most of those who insist upon using this version of the creation story to refute the theory of evolution do not see the sky as a dome that separates a watery level above us from a watery level below, or argue against the sun, moon, and stars as sources of the light we see.

In most cases, we do not treat the first chapter of Genesis as a way to understand science. For some reason, though, there are a couple of things that some Christians believe should be taken literally: a six-day creation is one; gender identity is another. However, if we are free to understand parts of the story figuratively—to say, for example, that there is not a layer of water above the sky from which rain originates—why should we insist that other parts must be understood literally? Although the people who told this creation story used the best ideas and knowledge of their time to convey important truths, these truths were about human beings and our relationship with God and the rest of the created order, not about science as we in our time understand science. In fact, this six-day creation cycle is not the only creation story in the Bible; the second chapter of Genesis tells a creation story that differs in significant ways. If there are two distinctly different versions of the creation story, then trying to take one version literally does not make sense. How do we choose which one is factual when both are equally a part of our Bible?

I do not have the time nor the space in this book to get into the science of hermeneutics, which is the way that we interpret what we read. That's a book in and of itself. I will note, however, that all of us interpret everything we read or hear. If you have ever had a misunderstanding with a friend or loved one, you know how easy it is for what one person says to be misunderstood by another, even when the speaker is working hard to be clear. Think about how the difficulties increase when you are with strangers or people from another culture, or even just people of another political persuasion. Think about how often people seem to talk past each other.

All of these difficulties are present when we read a text, with the additional challenges that arise from a text written in a different language, from a different culture, and from more than a thousand years ago. People's understanding of the world was different; they lived a reality unfamiliar to us. They had different assumptions, things they did not feel the need to say because everybody would have "known that," or assumed that something was obvious without stating it. As a result, it is literally impossible to do a "literal" interpretation of the Bible. We make assumptions about what we read. In the best case, we are aware of what assumptions we are making. What follows is my interpretation of the first creation story, along with my reasoning and assumptions. The reader can decide if my assumptions make sense to them and to their own experience of the world and of the way God is at work in it.

One hermeneutical way of determining the meaning of biblical passages is to look at other passages in the Bible that talk about the same subject. Although that sometimes leads to apparent contradictions, if one believes the Bible is a record of God's dealings with human beings and that God is consistent (even when human beings are not), then looking at a wider selection of passages may shed light on more obscure meanings. This common hermeneutical technique is called *Gezerah shavah* in Jewish biblical interpretation.[33] The obvious parallel passage is the second creation account, found in the second chapter of Genesis.

The first thing to note about the creation of human beings in the second creation story is that a single human being (or "earth-creature" in Hebrew) was created at the beginning of the story. The word used does not denote a gendered being in Hebrew. This earth-creature was not the pinnacle of creation, but was created first so there would be a steward, or caretaker, for the rest of creation that came later. In spite of all the variety of life, especially human life, however, the earth-creature was alone. It was the only one of its kind. So God creates another

---

[33] Jewish Virtual Library, "Hermeneutics," accessed March 24, 2017, http://www.jewishvirtuallibrary.org/hermeneutics.

earth-creature. In this creation, which happens differently, gender appears. The ungendered earth-creature becomes two gendered human beings. Rather than being an absolute necessity for humans to be gendered, gender seems to be an afterthought: a way of dealing with human loneliness, a way to help people feel connected to one another. Sender Rozesz, an attorney with a background in adult Jewish pluralistic education, argues that "so long as they were bound up in a single body, perfect they were, but they were missing the passion, the fire; the ability to separate as though they don't belong together—but then come together in the most intimate of ways."[34]

According to the second story, it was a rib that was taken from the first earth-creature to make the second. I have encountered Christians who believe that men have fewer ribs than women. (In case you did not know, both have twelve sets *pair* of ribs. Occasionally an individual will have eleven sets or thirteen, but not because of gender.) We have, therefore, the story of the taking of a rib from the original earth-creature that made that person into a man, and the giving of that rib to a second earth-creature that made that one into a woman. If we were treating the story literally—which I am not advocating— we would have to explain how ribs cause gendering and gender changes. We might decide that the writer or writers of Genesis had made a mistake about the part of the body that was removed. If you wanted to make a creature with biological parts corresponding to the female sex, you would have to transfer the uterus, vagina, and ovaries. If you were removing a part of the original earth-person to make them have the biological parts corresponding to the male sex, it would have needed to already

---

[34] Sender Rozesz, "Sex . . . In the Beginning," Jewrotica.com, October 17, 2014, http://jewrotica.org/2014/10/sex-in-the-beginning/.

possess a penis and testicles. The original earth-creature would have needed sexual organs of both biological sexes to begin with.[35] A person with organs corresponding to both biological sexes is intersex: the first earth-creature would have needed to be one of the forms of intersex to make the story work as it is told in the second chapter of Genesis—a very different result from the first creation story. Justin Tanis argues, "If completeness comes from having both male and female, then a person who possessed both is a return to the original completion in the earth creature."[36]

How, then, are we to understand gender in our tradition when we have one story in which humans are made gendered, and a second story in which an agender or intersex person was made first and later split into two gendered beings? At the very least, I think we have to concede that maybe our ancestors in the faith did not think that God was as concerned about gender as we are. Perhaps, as we have seen historically, they were more aware than many are in this day and age of the fact that there are not just two perfect and separate genders, and that a binary understanding of gender was not God's original and unbreakable will for creation, which seems to be the case in the animal world, as we have previously noted.

Tanis argues the creation story presents other binaries that are not exclusive.[37] For example, only day and night were created, but not twilight or dawn. Dry land and water were supposedly separated, but we also have marshes and swamps where dry land and water mix. Just because marshes or twilight are not mentioned in creation does not mean that either is impossible

---

[35] Tanis, 61.

[36] Ibid.

[37] Ibid., 57–58.

or was excluded. The binaries were meant to suggest not only the extremes that are named, but everything in between. If that is the case with dawn and with swamps, why exclude the possibility of that also being true in the case of gender?

The Purpose of the Creation Stories

If the creation stories are not exact descriptions of events and they are not science textbooks, how do we understand that which we honor as sacred scripture and the word of God? Although Rabbi Jonathan Sacks is writing for a Jewish audience, I think that he describes a way of understanding the texts that makes sense in light of what we know about how they were written and how they have been used across the millennia by both Christians and Jews.

> Because, if the book [Genesis] that begins with the words *Bereishit bara elokim* is called by us Torah, and if Torah is the name of a genre, it is telling us what kind of book it is, and Torah means teaching, or it means instruction, or it means, in the largest sense of the word, law— then Torah is, as I said before, an answer to a very specific question. Not the question, What is the case? How did the world come into being?—facts. But an answer to the question, How shall I live?[38]

---

[38] Jonathan Sacks, "Faith Lectures—Creation: Where Did We Come From?" RabbiSacks.org (blog), February 6, 2001, rabbisacks.org/faith-lectures-creation-where-did-we-come-from/.

To see these writings not as science textbooks, but as stories that help us know how to live, frees us up to interpret them in ways that accord with their purpose. We do not have to force a literal understanding on the texts. Instead, we are invited to think about why these stories were important to those who told them, wrote them, and passed them down through the centuries.

The great sweep of the creation story was meant to place human beings in the scheme of God's magnificent act of creation, and to position humankind as unique among creatures as being made in the image and likeness of God. We possess something of the divine, giving us incredible worth and value, and this worth and value is not to be confined to one gender; they encompass male and female. However, like the description of day and night, we do not have to argue that male and female mean only male and female; they can also encompass all that falls between what is named. Male and female may have been the storytellers' way of indicating all people, just as day and night meant all parts of the day, and water and dry land meant all parts of our world. That means we need to honor all people, whatever their gender identity, because all of us—men and women, trans* and cis, straight and gay, gender conforming and gender queer—are important parts of God's creation. All of us are of great value as beings made in the image and likeness of God. In our next chapter, we will look at this God whom we image, a God who is beyond our binary categories of gender.

CHAPTER 4

Describing a Non-Binary God

Trinitarian Theology and Gender

How do we understand God in a world in which trans* people are a part of creation? If we take seriously the proposition that all humans are made in the image and likeness of God, then to say the presence of trans* people in our communities does not have an effect upon our understanding of God is to suggest (subtly or maybe not so subtly) that the humanity of some represents God's image and likeness better than that of others. It is a tactic used throughout human history to designate certain people as not fully human or, at least, somehow not as able to share in the dignity and respect that should be due to all who share God's image and likeness.

However, our God is not a simple deity, or even one deity among other deities. For Christians, God is both three and one simultaneously. We describe God as a Trinity. This doctrine is so central to our understanding as Christians that we have a Sunday dedicated to it on our church calendar, although it is not the favorite Sunday of most of the preachers I know. We cannot define or exactly describe the Trinity, and this is not a new problem. Efforts to closely and rationally describe God were at the heart of many of the controversies of the earliest era of Christian history. Instead of a clear description of God, what they handed down was some odd nomenclature and a set of assertions that seem contradictory as well. A story told about a missionary—probably fictional—says he tried to describe the Trinity to some people who had never heard of Christianity. They were puzzled and, scratching their heads, replied, "Holy Father, we understand. Holy Son, we understand. Holy Bird, we do not understand!" The same can be said to be true of many Christians.

Although the doctrine of the Trinity has been a subject of controversy from the earliest days of Christianity, a new concern has arisen in our time. The traditional way of naming God as Father, Son, and Holy Spirit is troubling for many people, both because of the names used and because of the ways in which we understand the relationships between the members of the Trinity. As noted in the story above, it can sometimes seem like we are talking about two men and a bird. If humans are made in the image and likeness of God, then what does it mean that there are no feminine images of God in the Godhead? Does that mean that women or trans* people or intersex or gender queer people do not reflect the image and likeness of God, or that they reflect it in an inferior way? If we take Genesis 1:26–28 seriously, men and women together reflect the image of God, but in no place in our traditional way of referring to God is there anything that sounds remotely female. Some Christian traditions try to claim the divine feminine in other ways, all of which are problematical. Some use feminine pronouns when talking of the Holy Spirit, as the Hebrew word for spirit, *ruach*, is feminine. Hebrew, like many other languages (but not English), attributes gender to all nouns. However the concept of *ruach* was translated into the Greek of the Christian scriptures, the word *pneuma*, which is neuter in gender, was used. Sociologists have seen the elevation of Mary into co-redemptrix and queen of heaven in some branches of Christianity as another way in which some Christians have attempted to address the lack of the divine feminine. While Mary may indeed be closer to God than other human beings, she is not divine, leaving men to image God and women to image a faithful woman.

The second issue that is often raised about our understanding of the Trinity, particularly by theologians in the various liberation traditions, is the relationship between the members of the Trinity. Are they all equal in power and godliness, or is the Father somehow the preeminent person of the Trinity, to whom all other members are subject, or to whom Christ is subject while the Holy Spirit is subject to both the Father and Son? The idea that the Father is at the head of the Trinity is often described as the monarchy of the Father. It is a major concern in Eastern Orthodox traditions, but it also pops up, even if in a somewhat hidden fashion, among contemporary Western theologians as they argue for a more communal and egalitarian understanding of the Trinity. The words Father and Son tend to take on connotations of human father and son relationships; the norm of patriarchy is that the son is to be subservient and obedient to the father. (Although most theologians will note that earthly fathers and sons should base their relationship upon the divine one, humans often go in the other direction. Since we feel more comfortable describing our experiences of human father/son relationships, far too often we make the divine relationship the image of the human one, not vice versa.)

The ways in which we describe God as Trinity are complicated, usually patriarchal (emphasizing traditional hierarchical familial roles), excluding all genders except male, and highly contested. Modern systematic theologians attempt to deal with the ways that the Trinity has been used to uphold patriarchal roles and to subordinate women, while, at the same time, they attempt to preserve traditional understandings of God (and in many cases, traditional language as well). There is often a split between feminist theologians and more traditional systematic theologians—who have been predominantly men—about the ways we need to rethink the Trinity in order to minimize the ways in which our description of God has served to elevate one gender: by identifying God with a specific gender and by excluding representations of God that reflect other gender identities. While the absence of the feminine is the concern most often voiced by feminist theologians, many gay and lesbian theologians critique traditional descriptions of the Trinity for the ways that they use heterosexual models, either explicitly or implicitly, to uphold their understanding. Delving into gender and sexual orientation with respect to the Trinity is a minefield, yet I feel a need to offer something to demonstrate the way in which the acceptance of a broader range of human gender identities can broaden our understanding of God.

I am not a systematic theologian by training, so I will rely on two who are and who have written about gender in respect to the Trinity. Sarah Coakley is a British Anglican theologian who, while maintaining a fairly traditional understanding of the Trinity, gave me a glimpse of a way of understanding the Trinity that, if taken seriously, demonstrates how trans* people can help us to better image God. The second is Linn Marie Tonstad, an American who critiques Coakley's model for the way it still reinforces binary gender and gender roles. Unfortunately, neither of these theologians deals with the issue of gender identity. However, their ideas about gender and sexuality provide a foundation for a theology for trans* allies.

Sarah Coakley and the Non-Binary God

In acknowledging the ways in which our attempts to describe the Trinity have been gendered and the ways in which that gendering has been used to support the subordination of women, Coakley sounds like many feminist theologians. She acknowledges the danger this structured hierarchy "could combine naturally at the symbolic level with other biblically sanctioned forms of subordination: the church's subordination to Christ, woman's subordination to man, children's or slaves' subordination to the *paterfamilias*."[1] However, unlike many feminist theologians, she does not give up on traditional understandings of gender or reduce the gendering that is present in those depictions of God. She is trying to walk a fine line between traditional understandings (often expressed in intentionally patriarchal terminology and imbued with culturally determined gender roles by two thousand years of Christian history) and contemporary challenges to those roles and their supporting doctrine by modern gender theory.

When many feminist theologians reject heavily gendered understandings of the Trinity, why is Coakley so insistent upon maintaining them? She argues that "gender matters," because

---

[1] Sarah Coakley, *God, Sexuality, and the Self* (Cambridge: Cambridge University Press, 2013), 154.

it is an essential part of what it means to be human. Human life is inherently about "differentiated, embodied relationship," and "to fail to chart the differences and performances of gender would be to ignore one of the most profound aspects of human experience."[2] In response to feminist critiques that suggest that traditional understandings of the Trinity are fatally flawed by centuries of patriarchal thought, Coakley suggests that we upend our notions of the Trinity. Instead of beginning with the Father, which leads to a very hierarchical description, Coakley argues that we need to reclaim the priority of the Spirit in our understanding of God, for it is the Spirit who is primarily responsible for incorporating us into the life of the Trinity.

Theologies beginning with the Spirit have not always been appreciated in the Church. Unlike Trinitarian theologies that begin with the Father, which tend to stress the importance of hierarchy and subordination, as well as reason and tradition, those elements of our tradition that have emphasized the role of the Spirit are much more unruly, and those individuals who have championed the role of the Spirit have often been labeled heretics or mystics (or sometimes both—usually heretics while alive and mystics later). The loosening of the life of God's people from authoritarian structures has given us powerful and important moments of growth and transformation, but at the cost of loss of control over the results. In general, the Church has preferred a more stable and controlled state than the often chaotic challenge of living fully in the Spirit. There is an old joke about Episcopalians, from the days when the charismatic movement was gaining strength in the Episcopal Church, that contains more than a little truth: "If something unusual is going to happen in the service, Episcopalians want a rubric (in other

---

2 Ibid., 53.

words, a liturgical direction) that says, 'it will happen at this point.'"

How, then, does giving priority to the Holy Spirit disrupt the gender binary? "It is the very threeness of God, I shall argue, transformatively met in the Spirit, which gives the key to a view of gender that is appropriately founded in bodily practices of prayer," Coakley answers.[3] By giving the Spirit equal voice with the Father and Son, it disrupts that binary, reminding us that the heart of God is one and three, but never two, and therefore challenges all binaries. The focus shifts from the male father/ son relationship to something more complex, and this complexity has implications for humans made in the likeness of God. *"Twoness, one might say, is divinely ambushed by threeness."*[4] In spite of the potential for affirming a variety of genders in this focus upon the threeness of God, however, Coakley is unwilling to completely give up the gender binary. She argues that "the interruptive work of the trinitarian God does not obliterate the twoness of gender."[5] In doing so, she reaffirms, although perhaps unintentionally, the very gender binary that she is seeking to disrupt. In the final section of this chapter, I will comment on the possibilities I can see for a non-binary understanding of gender that she has not explored.

If the threeness of God is supposed to disrupt the twoness of gender without destroying its essential binary nature, what has it actually accomplished? Rather than challenging the binary understanding of human gender, Coakley talks about it as making gender "labile," not static. As one encounters the Holy Spirit through prayer, one's understanding and performance

---

[3] Ibid., 34.
[4] Ibid., 58.
[5] Ibid., 57.

of gender is not static or stuck, but "subject to endless refor-
mulations." In essence, although Coakley argues that this disrupts the gender binary (while simultaneously not destroying
that binary), what she is really arguing is not a disruption of
the gender binary but a disruption of societally imposed gender
roles. Throughout Christian history, those who were most com-
mitted to prayer and contemplation found cultural gender
norms too confining when they were being transformed by the
Spirit, and their transformation required both a "renegotiation
of gender" roles and a "release from societally mandated roles."[6]
Such disruption of gender roles can be a necessary and welcome
relief for those whose lives have been limited.

While Coakley's theology of the Trinity opens up an interesting space with its idea of the lability of gender, her discussion of its effect on human gender retains two problematic areas
for our discussion of a theology that recognizes and celebrates
gender beyond the binary. First, it keeps gender within the
Godhead. In her need to maintain traditional understandings
of the Trinity, she leaves intact the Father/Son relationship at its
heart. In raising the importance of the Spirit, she does challenge
the primacy of that relationship, but we still have masculinity
privileged by its place in the Trinity. Second, she reaffirms the
nature of human gender as binary. I will address both of these
concerns in the final section of this chapter, but first I want to
add another voice to the conversation.

---

[6] Ibid., 132.

Gender and the Trinity
from a Lesbian Point of View

In her book *God and Difference: The Trinity, Sexuality, and the Transformation of Finitude,* Linn Marie Tonstad tells about her decade-long attempt to combine Trinitarian theology with her experience as a feminist and a lesbian. As she read other theologians, Tonstad found that even LGBT-friendly theologians' attempts to describe the Trinity were done in ways that still valued sexual difference and reinforced traditional gender roles and values. "Even queer-friendly and feminist theologians who attempt this often repeat and sometimes heighten the historical proclivity of Christianity to encode masculinism and (symbolic) heterosexuality within a trinitarian logic."[7] I chose Tonstad as the second voice in our conversation for two reasons. First, she critiques several contemporary theologians, including Sarah Coakley, whom we discussed in the previous section. Second, I included her because of her identity as a queer woman and as a radical feminist, which means that rather than trying, as Coakley does, to reconcile experience with tradition, Tonstad does the reverse: she starts with lived experience and uses it to critique the tradition. As she notes, "The argument of this book is informed by anti-inclusive, antinormative, and antiequality queer critiques and radical (rather than equality or difference) feminism."[8] Culture teaches all of us what is important and what is normal. We tend to repeat what we have been taught uncritically, and we often do not even notice the assumptions that undergird our arguments or beliefs. It is especially important to listen to voices from communities that have been marginalized

---

[7] Linn Marie Tonstad, *God and Difference: The Trinity, Sexuality, and the Transformation of Finitude* (New York: Routledge, 2016), 1.

[8] Ibid., 3.

because those of us who do not share their experiences are often blind and deaf to the ways in which language and assumptions have been shaped to exclude those who do not fit into traditional narratives. One disadvantage in using Tonstad is that she is focused more upon sexual orientation than gender identity. I will argue, however, that Tonstad's critique about the ubiquity of an assumed heteronormative (assuming that heterosexuality is normal) framework can also be extended to the underlying assumptions of binary gender, particularly in Coakley's work.

As Tonstad notes, Coakley is one feminist whose work is actually considered mainstream in the academic world of theology. Often, feminist theologians (as well as theologians from other marginalized groups) are brought in as examples of theological discourse that would only be applicable to a small group— unlike the work of traditional theologians (most often white males) who are assumed to be writing "objective" or "universal" theology. With her critique of other feminist theologians, as well as her adherence to traditional understandings and to the academically valued "shared rationality and analytic philosophy of religion," Coakley's work is considered to be on par with other "traditional" academic theologians by those same theologians.[9]

Even though theologians acknowledge that complete objectivity is impossible—all of us see things from our own perspective—the pretense is still highly valued by academics. However, this "objectivity" tends to reflect not a universal human experience of God, but the God experienced by white, well-educated, middle- to upper-class, straight, cis men, whose understandings have been implicitly considered to be the "norm" for all people. Others, such as Coakley, who do not embody the traditional type of academic theologian, may choose to join that way of looking at the world

---

[9] Ibid., 98.

(for that is often highly rewarded in academia). Unfortunately, it also carries with it unspoken and often unnoticed assumptions about what is true and how the world works.

Tonstad critiques Coakley's work for the way that her arguments still assume a patriarchal and heterosexual world as the norm. She argues that, rather than reducing the hierarchical understandings of gender, Coakley reinforces the symbolic and theological understandings of gender that have undergirded Western notions of gender hierarchy. The appropriate stance for Christians is still that of a female—vulnerable and submissive—toward a male God. The combining of traditional gender roles with the human-divine relationship, which is inherently hierarchical, does nothing to weaken cultural gender hierarchies,[10] but instead the equating of God with males and humans with females has been one way that these gender hierarchies have been maintained throughout Christian history.

In addition, Tonstad critiques Coakley for assuming that sex is automatically the heterosexual act of penetration. She argues that "moving between 'male' phallicism and 'feminine' receptive activity does nothing to undo either their human ordering in relation to each other or the primary heterosexism that such imagery encodes."[11] Instead, Tonstad offers the image of sex as touch without penetration as one way not only to avoid the hierarchical gender relations that bedevil Trinitarian theology, but also to lead to a strong basis for the Trinity as a communion into which we are invited.[12]

Coakley is not unaware of the dangers inherent in Trinitarian language, admitting that "no doctrine of the Trinity, as charter

---

[10] Ibid., 104.
[11] Ibid., 105.
[12] Ibid., 232.

and paradigm of perfect *relationship*, can be completely inno-
cent of political, familial, and sexual associations."[13] Instead of
changing language, however, Coakley argues that in contemplative practice, the Christian comes to learn what words like
"Father" really mean, and that through the higher states of contemplation, the Christian will be able to achieve the "demanding
and complicated renegotiation of gender (and simultaneously a
release from societally mandated roles)."[14] In other words, individual Christians, through their practices of prayer, can learn
to recognize the "wrong" understanding of gender and gender
roles, resisting them in their own lives. This, however, leads to
a major problem. It leaves this wrong understanding of gender
and gender roles active, and even dominant, both in the culture
and in the Church.[15] Unless everyone reaches these high levels
of contemplation, most will have no access to more enlight-
ened ideas. This is not acceptable in a world in which traditional Christian understandings of gender and gender roles are
causing uncountable harm to those whose understanding of
their gender identity and whose ways of expressing that gender
do not neatly fit into traditional understandings.

We cannot leave unchallenged the traditional understandings
of gender and gender roles, because of the danger they pose to
some of God's children. As Christians we are called to reach out
to all, to honor all, and to protect those whom society has tar-
geted for harm, particularly when such harm is often done in
the name of Christ. We cannot rely upon individuals to come

---

[13] Coakley, 266.

[14] Ibid., 132.

[15] As Tonstad notes, "the specific term *father* has shown itself as a potent inflammation
to Christian practices of gendered hierarchies, especially in combination with the
theological significance often given to the maleness of Christ and his disciples."
Tonstad, 200.

to a correct understanding of gender and gender roles through high-level contemplation. We must confront the inequities and injustices perpetrated by Christian theology, whether we believe they are due to a misrepresentation of that theology or to its natural outgrowth. To do so, we need not simply a denunciation of the misuse of our fundamental symbols, but a theology that puts forth a more loving and true version of what it means to be children of God. In the next section, I offer some ideas of things that I think should be a part of such a theology.

Creator Spirit

Sustainer

Toward a Non-Binary Theology

Introduction

Most Christians do not pay a lot of attention to arguments about the Trinity. Many believe that the ideas contained in the classic formulations of the Trinity, drawn as they were from Greek and Roman philosophical ideas of the early centuries of the Common Era, seem as disconnected from the lives they live as medieval arguments about how many angels could dance on the head of a pin. Why should we bother with descriptions of the Trinity? Why do they matter anymore? They obviously mattered in the third and fourth centuries CE when councils were called to debate and people were condemned and exiled as a result, often only to return from exile with the next change of emperor. It mattered so much that the Roman Emperor Constantine (who was not baptized as a Christian until his deathbed) convened the Council of Nicaea to stop all of the infighting among Christians because it was disturbing the peace of his empire. He wanted a single, universally agreed-upon faith, instead of the variety of Christian beliefs and practices that characterized the earliest years of Christian history, and he would impose that agreement upon all in the empire.

For those early Christians, these discussions about the nature of God, Jesus, and the Spirit, as well as their interrelationship, mattered greatly. They knew what we have perhaps forgotten: what we believe has consequences not only for how we worship, but also for how we live our lives in imitation of Christ. Who Christ is, how Christ relates to the God worshiped by the Jews, and where the Spirit fits in are of ultimate importance. They were trying to craft a new understanding of God, a more complex God. It would not be a strict monotheistic faith, in the same way as Judaism or Islam, for it would have these three persons. However, it would definitely not be a polytheistic faith, like those of most of the cultures that surrounded them. They would identify more with the Jewish faith, as that was the faith of Jesus and his original followers, but they needed new language to express their understandings, and the language of Greek philosophical thought proved to be best suited for the task.

The compromises that they made in their language were carefully crafted, so as not to allow people to go too far in either direction from the central understandings of the newly agreed-upon faith. However, language, no matter how carefully crafted, is always imprecise, particularly about subjects such as God and relationships within the Godhead. How can we imagine that we can really describe who God is within God's self? The early Trinitarian theologians acknowledged the fact that the true nature of God was always more than we can express in language, and at some point, language had to give way to the silence appropriate to mystery. We cannot, and should not, try to pin God down or to box God in, for God is incapable of being either pinned down or boxed in. Unfortunately, such humility has not always been a part of the art and practice of theology.

At too many times and in too many places, theologians have lost that sense of humility—thundering instead that they, and they alone, know who God was and what God required of God's people. When humans are tempted to speak as if they are God's personal spokespeople, we can usually be sure it is not the love of God accepted in great humility that is driving them. Far too often, it is their own ideas, entrenched cultural norms, or unexamined teachings that are given "God's sanction."

Theology matters. It matters as Christians try to live out their lives in accordance with the God they encounter. It also matters because Christian theology has been too often used to uphold bias, hate, and the oppression of people who do not fit into cultural norms that supposedly have the backing of Christian belief. The treatment of LGBTQIA+ people, particularly trans* people, has been fueled by a theology that seems to sanction hatred and violence against them. For instance, conversion therapy—abusive programming that promises to make someone straight—is, after all, most often run and supported by Christians who believe that they are acting in Christian love to save people from the wrath of God. Those who commit violence against LGBTQIA+ people will often use justifications from Christian theology to paint themselves as the "good guys." Theology matters because it touches the deepest parts of human existence: not only our relationship with God, but also how we view our relationships with those around us. We need a theology that can help us to love more fully, as Christ loves us.

Names for God

The Bible offers many images of God. Some are personal, such as king or advocate. Some are more impersonal, such as crag or stronghold. Some come from nature, such as hen or eagle. With the codifying of the Trinitarian formula, Father, Son, and Holy Spirit became the preeminent image. Like all of the others mentioned above, however, it is still only an image of a God who is beyond all that we can possibly imagine. Although the terms are meant to suggest a relational connection, the almost exclusive use of these names for the persons of the Trinity has led to the enshrinement of hierarchy not only within God but in human relationships as well. By enshrining the Fatherhood in God (and with a complete absence of any feminine imagery in God), we have allowed theology to be co-opted into upholding both hierarchy and patriarchy.

I advocate for a return to using a multitude of images of God. It may be, at least at present, that the image of Father is too emotionally freighted to be a useful way to portray God for many people. Not only is it off-putting for many women, but it also can be a troubling image for any who have had difficult relationships with their own fathers. Abuse, neglect, and abandonment by their fathers can make it difficult for people to come close to the God whom we proclaim is Love. Although some people find that imaging God as Father can help them heal from a painful parental relationship, many others are reluctant after their experiences to trust another "Father."

I would like to focus in this theology on the names suggested by Tonstad. She suggests that "The Spirit is the Power of God, the Son is the Glory of God, and the Father is the Name of God, which is Love."[16] By not using human figures to stand in for God, there is less of a temptation to idolatry: confusing the figure with that for which it stands. The names still connote relationship, but they are not given in accordance with faulty human relationships; they do not elevate one relationship over

---

[16] Ibid., 231.

any other. While non-personal names for God can make God feel disconnected from us and our concerns, the declaration that the Name of God is Love, besides having ample scriptural support, indicates that God is very much active in our lives and the life of all creation. It also grounds all creation in the Name of Love, a Love that is powerful and glorious. Tonstad argues that "as an expression of God's love for material creation," the God who is Love within the community of the Trinity also reaches out in love and unites with creation in such a way that matter is transformed, but not destroyed.[17]

Traditional theologians often argue against attempts to refer to God with feminine names by saying that God is not gendered. However, if God is not gendered, then we do not need to express the relationships between the persons of the Trinity in gendered ways. Non-gendered language for God removes the foundation for many arguments about men's superiority and women's inferiority. It also helps to reduce human focus upon the gender of others (in the name of God) and allows people to express gender in a multitude of ways that do not require them to identify only with one gender and its associated gender roles. By praying in the Name of Love, the Glory of Love, and the Power of Love, we open ourselves to a larger understanding not only of God, but of humans, who are made in God's image.

Relationships in the Trinity

Coakley notes that the linear understanding of the Trinity, in which the Father is supreme, the Son is second in the hierarchy, and the Spirit is a far distant third, "could combine naturally at the symbolic level with other biblically sanctioned forms of

---

[17] Ibid., 232.

subordination,"[18] and argues that it was this incorrect understanding of the relationships within the Trinity that was the
source of gender hierarchies, not the use of the terms Father and
Son. She notes that within Christian history, groups that ele-
vated the importance of the Spirit (as she suggests we should do)
were less likely to support gendered hierarchies (in other words,
they were more able to affirm female leadership). Such a way
of relating to the Trinity has been seen, however, to have both
political and sexual overtones, from the early Christian writings
all the way to the present.[19] While mystics and contemplatives
naturally moved in this direction, those most concerned with
Church order tended to suppress the valuing of the Spirit equally
within the Trinity. Coakley argues that no change needs to be
made in the traditional formulations of the Trinity for those
who accord the Spirit its proper place; people involved in the
higher reaches of contemplative prayer will come to understand
the Trinity rightly and act upon the correct understanding.

One of the pieces of art that Coakley uses to describe this
more egalitarian relationship among the persons of the Trinity
is a fifteenth-century Russian icon painted by Andrei Rublev.
Usually called *the Trinity*, it officially portrays the three angels
who visited Abraham to announce that Sarah would have
a son,[20] a Hebrew Bible story often invoked to show that the
idea of the Trinity was present even during the time before the
coming of Jesus (in Rublev's time, it was forbidden to picture
God the Father, hence the illustrating of the Abraham story
instead). A picture of this icon is shown on the following page.

---

[18] Coakley, 154.
[19] Ibid., 121.
[20] Gen. 18:1–13.

There are several noteworthy features that make this image useful for our theology for trans* allies. First, the figures are androgynous: they are not obviously either male or female. This decreases the focus upon the normally gendered representations of the first two persons of the Trinity. The second interesting feature is that it is not immediately obvious which figure is intended to represent which person of the Trinity. Often, in Trinitarian art, the Father is given the highest place, but in this case, the "Father" does not actually occupy that position. Third, the three persons are shown sitting in a way that emphasizes their essential equality, reducing the hierarchical focus of most

Trinitarian writing and art.[21] (Henri Nouwen notes that the front of the table has an opening to allow us to enter into this gathering as well.)[22] This egalitarian image is a starting place for a description of the Trinity in a theology for trans* allies. The lack of gender signifiers, the very egalitarian way the persons are depicted, and the openness to those who are viewing it are all useful. It is the Trinity not as a king's court, but as a community that is radically open to all.

While Coakley speaks favorably of this icon, I agree with Tonstad's critique that Coakley's own descriptions of the relationships within the Trinity do not depict such an egalitarian fellowship. Having the persons of the Trinity be male in relation to those below them, and female in relation to those above them, still reinforces both the above/below binary and the stereotypical associations of femininity with passivity and masculinity with activity.[23] In describing the relationships between the persons of the Trinity, as well as the relationship between God and humans, Coakley follows the tradition of using sexual activity—one of the most intimate ways of human relating—as the metaphor. There is nothing inherently wrong with using sexuality for that metaphor, but, as Tonstad has noted, Coakley has a narrow definition of sexual activity: heterosexual sexual activity in which an active male penetrates a receptive female. This insistence upon identifying only heterosexual penetrative sex as a suitable metaphor is one thing that makes it difficult for Coakley to free herself of the gendered hierarchy, as much

---

[21] If you are curious, the middle figure is the Son, pointing toward the Eucharistic bread. Two of the figures are gazing at the third, indicating that the Father is on the left, and the Spirit is therefore on the right. The only feature that indicates any hierarchy is that the gazes of the Son and Spirit both rest on the Father.

[22] Henri J.M. Nouwen, *Behold the Beauty of the Lord: Praying with Icons* (Notre Dame, IN: Ave Maria Press, 1987), 24.

[23] Tonstad, 105.

as she may wish to claim that all persons of the Trinity need to be equal. Tonstad argues that a broader understanding of sexuality may solve this problem by replacing penetrative, reproductive sexuality with a sexuality that is based upon touch, and in which partners exist in a more equal relationship. Since the Trinity is the preeminent symbol of communal life, it allows us to picture community in a way where we can be together "in the same place at the same time—as it were—without shattering, breaking, emptying, or penetrating, through the transformation of materiality that comes from God's unitive and assimilative love of mattered creation."[24] This is an understanding of God that is open enough to welcome the variety of people made in the image and likeness of God, and it is a vision, like that of Rublev's *Trinity*, of a community inscribed not with hierarchical relationships but with the more complicated and life-giving relationships characterized by love between equals.

Made in the Image and Likeness of God

If an image like Rublev's *Trinity* can depict the Trinitarian God without clearly defining gender and reinscribing gender roles, then defining gender or policing gender expression in those made in the image of God is not an essential function in Christian theology; the possibility of gender being expressed in an infinite variety of ways among those made in the image of God opens up. It does what any theology that takes the experience of trans* people seriously needs to do: it discards the binary basis for our understanding of gender.

For Coakley, the very threeness of God makes gender roles labile, but she insists upon leaving gender itself stuck in

---

24 Ibid., 237.

twoness.[25] There is nothing particularly necessary about binary gender, however, so I will take Coakley's argument to what I believe is its logical conclusion. Not only does the Spirit's three-ness make gender roles and gender presentation labile, it makes gender itself labile. What if the very idea of binaries is not a construct of God, but a construct of the human mind, an attempt to make a complex world "manageable"? What if what God is doing at this time is calling us to leave behind our simplistic under-standings of gender, just as we have been forced throughout Christian history to leave behind other overly simplified under-standings, and embrace the rich diversity with which God has blessed us? If we are made in the image and likeness of God who is one and three, but never two, how can we insist that we are made on a binary model?

[25] Coakley, 57.

CHAPTER 5

Toward a Theology for Trans* Allies

Binary Pairs in a Complex World

We live in a world of dizzying complexity, yet our language is filled with binary concepts. We live in a world far from simple, yet we often expect that many questions can be answered with only a "yes" or "no." If we listen to the way we speak, we might think we lived in a world of extremes and nothing in between: darkness and light, right and wrong, wet and dry, short and tall, big and little, hard and soft, smooth and rough, hot and cold. The list of opposing pairs with which we try to describe our world could go on and on. Binary pairs are useful for simplifying the large amount of information we are required to process. It is developmentally appropriate for young children to think in binary terms as they are learning to categorize their world, but most people eventually outgrow that phase.

Fortunately, most adults recognize that while sorting things into opposing categories can be a useful way of dealing with large amounts of information, not everything fits neatly into binary categories. Sometimes it is not a simple yes or no that is required to answer a question. Instead, our questions require more reasonable answers: "maybe," "probably not," or even "I don't know." Sometimes levels of illumination are neither completely dark nor completely light. Sometimes it is not easy to judge things as right or wrong; it can depend upon the situation —things might be both right and wrong at the same time. Sometimes temperatures are neither hot nor cold, but cool or lukewarm or tepid. Sometimes the same temperature feels cold to one person and hot to another. Most of us have learned that binaries are limiting and in many cases are inadequate to describe the world around us, often without even realizing that is what we have learned.

However, there are some binaries that seem to be difficult for us to let go of. Often, these are categories around identity: who is who, and how different groups are valued. Binaries around race and ethnicity can be such a category, leading to a devaluing of the worth of those labeled as "other." Beautiful and ugly, fat and thin, physically fit and out of shape, mentally healthy and mentally ill, people with disabilities and those currently abled, educated and uneducated, rich and poor: these binaries are much harder for us to ignore, as they serve to mark the boundaries between those who are like us and those who are not. Marketing, politics, and the legal system all tend to reinforce these markers of identity, privileging some at the expense of others. While many people fall between the extremes, we often act as if there is an obvious dividing line. One clear example is the way that people have been classified as black even when most of their ancestors were white. At one point in the history of the United States, it took only one drop of black blood to legally disqualify people from the privileges given to white people.

One of the hardest of these binaries to challenge is that between women and men. As I noted in earlier chapters, the need for people to have a clear, unambiguous, and unchanging gender was so important that intersex children were often subjected to numerous surgeries to make their genitals match the ideal of one of the two "acceptable" genders, even at the cost of both infertility and a loss of pleasure in sexual relationships as adults. Gender was often chosen, not on the basis of chromosomal makeup (as many people assume today), but by which way it was easier to make them "look normal." In practice, this meant many were assigned a female gender, as it was easier to shorten the tissue to clitoris length than to enlarge it to penis length. Through medical intervention and often strict rearing along gender lines, intersex children were pushed into the gender that others had decided "looked" right, whether or not they had the traditional chromosomal pattern for that assigned gender.

Why is this gender binary so difficult to challenge? I suggest there are four reasons. First, gender is one of the fundamental ways in which we classify and identify people. How many forms that require you to provide identification or personal information have *not* asked you for your gender? Probably very few. That question is found on all kinds of forms that have no need of this information. Still, for many years, it has been a reliable and (most of the time) easily ascertained bit of information. Even today, if you ask someone to describe another person, they are likely to begin with their gender. We are taught about gender from a very early age, and helped to learn to identify the gender of others by their outward appearance.

Second, the division of labor by gender has had a profound influence upon the way that we understand and relate to the concepts of women and men. In premodern cultures, while gender roles could be rigidly applied, labor was more communal, and the spheres of women's work and men's work often overlapped. In the modern era, men's work was valued more, since it brought in income and was done in the wider world. The work of maintaining home and family, which fell to women, was less valued because of its unpaid and private status.

Third, as is the case with many binaries, the categories of gender are not free of judgment. When we have paired categories, there is a strong tendency to decide which one is better. Some early cultures were (and some still are) matriarchal cultures where women have a dominant role in community life, and the deity or deities are often female. Western Christian culture, descended as it was from both the masculine desert god of the Hebrews and other male-centered cultures, privileged men. Female deities (or even a feminine character in the deity) were excluded and relegated to the agricultural cultures and religions present in the areas that the Hebrews were to conquer. A dominant masculine ideology has ruled the Western world up to the present, and that privileging of the male has been carried to more egalitarian or matriarchal societies elsewhere by way of conquest, colonization, and assimilation.

Few groups, having grown accustomed to a privileged and powerful place in society, willingly relinquish their perquisites and privileges. The initial battles for the way we understand and try to police culturally accepted gender roles and expression are far from over; we also face battles over our understanding of sexual orientation. Although these battles are ongoing, significant progress has been made on both fronts. Women have access to more jobs (although they are still paid less than men), educational opportunities, voting rights, and the ability to manage their own money. In many places (although not all), job discrimination against gays and lesbians is illegal, and the rights to marry and to adopt children were affirmed in major recent court victories. Trans* people, however, still do not have some of these same basic civil rights. In most states, it is legal to discriminate against trans* people, and their right to use public bathrooms is being contested in many places. As noted earlier, trans* people, particularly trans* people of color, are much more likely to be victims of violence, and far too many trans* teens live on the street, having been kicked out of their homes before finishing their education. Unemployment is higher in the trans* community than in society as a whole.

Fourth, restrictive gender roles and the concept of a binary gender have been undergirded by Christian theology. The combination of culture and religion, acting in concert to uphold binary gender and its accompanying gender roles, has been difficult to challenge. Although cis heterosexual women, gays, and lesbians have all suffered from an understanding of theology that uses masculinity and heterosexual reproductive sex to describe the Godhead, trans* people have been often vilified even by those who are supportive of women's changing roles and of civil rights for homosexuals. The challenge to the notion that there are two and only two genders that are completely distinct makes many people profoundly uncomfortable, and the trans* community has suffered greatly because of the discomfort of others. Although we cannot, through our theology, completely undo the discrimination against the trans* community, we have a responsibility to rework our theology to remove it as a continuing support for such discrimination and to reinforce it as support and advocacy for trans* people; we must work to make amends for the damage that has been done to them by Christian communities.

explainable myth story (handwritten margin note)

myth (handwritten margin note)

A Theological Rationale for Trans* Allies

According to the book of Genesis, human beings are made in the image and likeness of God. That statement is followed by the words, "male and female God created them." Those additional words have been used to support distinct gender roles throughout Christian history. Genesis 1:26–28 is one of the passages most often used to support the idea of gender complementarity —the idea that men and women are created for different roles, roles based not upon their personal gifts or skills, but simply upon their physical anatomy. It assumes an unchanging idea of gender roles throughout history and across geography. However, the idea of universal, unchanging gender roles cannot be supported by rigorous historical analysis or anthropological evidence. A close study of these fields demonstrates that the ways in which gender and gender roles have been understood have greatly changed due to cultural ideals and contexts. The idea of the nuclear family—two parents of different sexes and their children—that is so beloved of those who support rigid and unchanging gender roles is actually a modern invention.

I have argued that the key passage from Genesis 1:26–28 does not require the interpreter to assume that only two genders are available, any more than other pairs of words in this creation story, seen as opposites, exclude the states in between the extremes. I have also shown, through comparison of the two versions of the creation story, that gender is "queered" or made labile and unclear in these stories. How is one to understand gender when the original earth-person had "a rib" removed, which rendered that person suddenly male (instead of non-gendered), and the person made from that "rib" female?[1] While one could argue that this does not necessarily make the first earth-person

it's a myth (handwritten margin note)

---

[1] Gen. 2:21–22.

intersex, it definitely makes the gendering of humans in the biblical tradition odd or "queer." It means that gender, according to the creation story in the second chapter of Genesis[2] (probably the older of the two creation stories, according to scholars), is not part of God's original creation, but is something added later in order to make a fit companion for the original earth-creature, which gives credence to the idea that when the creation story in the first chapter of Genesis talks about humans being created in the image of God, male and female, the intent of that pronouncement is not to set up the idea of an immutable gender and accompanying gender roles. Instead, as in the case of day and night, or water and dry land, the terms male and female include not only the mentioned terms, but also all of the examples that fall somewhere in between. In adding the words about gender, the writers of the first creation story were expressing their belief that both men and women image God, a radical idea in a time when women were often seen as inferior, derivative, or even property. Their insistence upon naming the two genders seems to have been an attempt to expand those who were seen as being made in God's image, not narrow it.

What we know from our study of creation is its incredible diversity. Insects account for about 80 percent of the known species of animals, and approximately 900,000 species have been described.[3] Scientists estimate there are more species of insects around us that have yet to be categorized than all those that have already been documented. If one were simply to look at the most diverse group, beetles, they would find more than 350,000 species, and scientists believe that there are many more

---

[2] Gen. 2:4b–25.

[3] Smithsonian Institution, "Buginfo: Numbers of Insects (Species and Individuals)," Si.edu, accessed July 7, 2017, https://www.si.edu/Encyclopedia_SI/nmnh/buginfo/bugnos.htm.

to be discovered.[4] Even among the larger animals, the variety within and across closely related species showcases the diversity of living things. Human beings surely share in the diversity of creation; just as gender is not neatly divided into two separate, distinct, and immutable groups within the animal kingdom, the same seems to be true in the species *homo sapiens,* or human beings. We, like the rest of creation, share in God's love of variety and diversity.

Human beings have developed ways to simplify the vast amount of information we receive. Otherwise, we might be too distracted to pay attention to the things that are most important. One of our most useful tools has been our ability to categorize, lumping together things that share similar characteristics, which can be helpful in understanding our world. We do not have to see every cat in the world in order to recognize an unknown creature as a cat. We do not have to encounter every form of chair in the world to recognize things designed for humans to sit upon. We do not have to see every kind of tree to recognize a tree when we see one. Those are categories that most of us have pretty well defined; when we see an object or being with certain characteristics we are able to place it in the proper category.

Of course, our categories do not always work. People have made some very unusual chairs over the years, chairs that do not have a seat and four identifiable legs. Some cats may actually look little like our ideal version of the animal. Hairless cats might cause us to either take a second look to confirm that they are cats or else redefine our category. When we find examples that do not fit our neatly defined categories, we have a choice: we

---

[4] University of California, Berkeley, "Case Study: Why So Many Beetles?" Understanding Evolution: Your One-Stop Source for Information on Evolution, accessed July 7, 2017, http://evolution.berkeley.edu/evolibrary/article/side_O_0/beetles_01.

can broaden our definitions in order to include the new examples, or we can exclude those things or creatures that do not quite fit. While categorizing is a powerful tool for organizing information, it is only partially useful in describing our world, for the world contains a variety of things that do not nicely fit in our categories. These outliers call us to hold categories with permeable or changeable boundaries rather than insist upon keeping strict boundaries and reject anything that challenges them.

Like a binary computer, our minds like those instances when we can define a category and its opposite. Men are not women. Dark is not light. Hot is not cold. Animals are not plants. Dogs are not cats. High is not low. While these are some of the first categories that we learn, and they provide a powerful way of equipping young children for language and for understanding, they are deceptively comforting. We might prefer a world where right and wrong are easily distinguished one from another. We might prefer to live in a world that is black and white, but as we grow and encounter more of the world, we become aware of the gray areas that do not fit easily into either category. I remember arguments about whether pandas were bears or raccoons, until scientists decided that the real issue was that not all those we called pandas were related to each other. Great pandas were indeed closer to bears, and red pandas were indeed closer to raccoons; in spite of being examples of the category "panda," the two do not really belong together. Sometimes we have to let go of previously useful categories when new information challenges the way that we categorize something or someone.

To acknowledge that the trans* community is part of God's creation is to acknowledge that our attempt to simplify humans into two and only two distinct and unchangeable genders no longer describes the full human experience. Actually, it never really did, but at this point in our history we are being confronted with the breakdown of one of our most dearly held binaries: male/female. How do we understand humanity being made in the image and likeness of God when we have to acknowledge that humans are much more complicated than we have often been willing to admit? Perhaps we have to be willing to explore the complexity of a God who is also non-binary.

Proclaiming a Non-Binary God

As noted in the previous chapter, Sarah Coakley reminds us that we worship a God who is never binary. God can be one or three but never two, which means, she argues, that binary gender roles (but not binary gender itself) are challenged by our non-binary God. I argue that a non-binary God equally challenges our attachment to a binary understanding of gender itself. In Coakley's writings (and that of most theologians), the Father and Son language normally used for the first two persons of the Trinity does not have an exact correspondence to the father/son language about human beings. It is clear that Coakley rejects any attempts to change the traditional Trinitarian language, claiming that through contemplative prayer the individual comes to understand how that language has been misused. I agree with Tonstad, however, that using traditional Trinitarian language has had, and continues to have, a problematic impact in our culture, even if the intention was not to reinforce gendered roles.

All descriptions of the Trinity have to use metaphorical language—no language could ever adequately describe God, and metaphors always invite consideration not only of similarities but also of differences between the metaphor and what it is describing. So in what ways is the Fatherhood of God similar to human fatherhood, and in what ways is it different? Human fatherhood has changed over human history, and the roles of fathers in the lives of their children have not remained static. Does that imply that the relationship between the Father and the Son in the Trinity is also changing? Unlike human fathers, the Father in the Trinity did not impregnate a female deity to father the Son. According to Christians' understandings of the Trinity, the Father and the Son existed from before creation, and the traditional Christian formulations of the Trinity exclude any naming of a female familial relationship. Human fathers are not able to beget sons on their own, so familial language has definite limitations when talking of the Trinity. How, then, is God the Father similar to human fathers? In power? In expecting obedience? Most theologians argue that you cannot transfer the power relationships within the Trinity onto human relationships: the type of power often seen in human relationships is not found in the Trinity. These are the arguments usually used to dismiss feminist theologians' arguments for avoiding the Father/Son language, but if these power dynamics, present in traditionally human hierarchical relationships, are not justified by the traditional language of the Trinity, how does this metaphor reflect what is similar between human fathers and the divine Father?

If we want to talk about an equal relationship among three "persons," would we not want to use the same kind of language for all three persons? To describe one relationship in familial terms but use other language for the relationship of the Father and Son to the Spirit is to put the Spirit in a different type of relationship with the other two persons, something that is difficult to reconcile with the idea that all three persons are equally God and all are One: the God family has a Father, a Son, and something that is not named in terms of its family relationships. Most humans who are part of a family name themselves after family relationships, even if they are only an "honorary" family member. Again, the differences between the God "family" of the Trinity and human families seem more visible than the similarities.

It makes sense, then, to affirm that God, as Christians understand God, is non-binary in many ways, and that gender is not a necessary part of God. Gendered relationships have been only one of the ways that Christians have tried to understand our God who is sometimes one and sometimes three, but never two. However, across Christian history, this particular metaphor of God has become the dominant one, making it more difficult to see the ways in which the familial language of the Trinity not only added gender to God but also reinforced the accompanying power relationships and cultural gender roles that are attached to similar human relationships. The traditional language of the Trinity—Father, Son, and Holy Spirit—is an important part of Christian history and has held a prominent role in Christian worship. However, it is time to once again expand the metaphors that we use to describe our God. We need to incorporate metaphors that are a part of the whole of Christianity's history and come up with new ways to express our understanding of God who is not male and never binary. Once we break the hold one particular metaphor has upon our understanding of God, we are freed to consider a God who is much more than any one metaphor can encompass, and much greater than the human mind can comprehend. We can face the task of theology—talking about God—with a great deal more humility, realizing that all our words, all our images, all our understandings of God are partial at best, for we are like the five blind men who wanted to explore the elephant.

In the traditional story, the blind men were taken to an elephant so that they could use their hands to "see" what it was. One man reached out his hand and felt a tusk. He said that an elephant was like a curved sword. Another man felt the large ears, exclaiming that the elephant was like a fan. The third man touched the side of the elephant and declared that the elephant was like a wall. A fourth felt a leg and said that an elephant was like a tree trunk. The final man felt the tail of the elephant, proclaiming that the elephant was like a rope. The blind men went home all thinking that they alone knew what an elephant really was like. Each was right, but only partially right, for each encountered only a small portion of the elephant.

We face something even greater than an elephant: God. We are like the blind men groping around, trying to make sense of the small part of God we have experienced, both individually and collectively. Like them, we often try to argue about others' ways of describing God, for they do not match our own. We often act as if we believe that our experience of the One who made heaven and earth is sufficient to fully describe God. This awareness of the vastness of God, so far beyond all human understanding, is why mystics and other lovers of God often lapse into silence in the face of God. Even if we need to put our understanding of God into words—there are definitely times and places that need our witness—we need to be careful to remember that our experience of God is partial and fragmentary and to speak with humility. If God is non-binary, it is hardly surprising that those made in God's image and likeness do not fall neatly into the binary categories that we use to make sense of our world. Here lies the basis for a theology for trans* allies: the simple acknowledgment, present throughout Christian history, that God is three or one, but never two, challenges all of the binaries that human beings are so fond of creating. Those who are made in God's image and likeness are also complex, and beyond our ability to know and understand. If we approach describing God with humility, perhaps we ought to approach describing those made in the image and likeness of God with humility as well. In our human diversity, in our inability to be completely described, in our inability to fit neatly into categories, we reflect the image and likeness of our God. Those who challenge us to look at the complexity of human life are not problems to be solved, but gifts of a loving God to help us to grow into a deeper understanding of ourselves and our non-binary God.

Implications for Faith Communities

The first Pride Celebration that I experienced was in Portland, Maine. After the parade there was a festival, with a variety of booths. One caught my attention and left me transfixed with hope for the church. Outside a tent was a sign that read:

Under that tent, I saw healing taking place, as the walls between church and the LGBTQIA+ community were breached. There is a lot of anti-religious feeling in the LGBT community, especially anti-Christian feeling, for Christian hands are not clean in response to the systematic persecution of those whose gender identity or sexual orientation did not match society's expectations. Many members of the LGBTQIA+ community have suffered a great deal of violence, persecution, and rejection in the name of "religion." Many have been ostracized from their homes or faith communities because of who they are or whom they love. Far too many have little reason to love the Christian community. If we are to respond to the needs of these people, then, like the First Congregational Church of South Portland, we need to acknowledge the complicity of Christian churches and Christian teaching in the persecution of those who dared to live their lives with integrity. We will need to ask for forgiveness from those whom our churches have so greatly wronged.

Many churches are becoming much more welcoming for members of the trans* community, and God knows we need to become more welcoming. But it is not enough simply to welcome. To welcome them into our congregations is to imply somehow that this is our church: we are the hosts and they are guests. To place them in the role of guests is to require them to behave in socially acceptable ways and to follow the rules of the house they are visiting. To welcome them as guests is to imply that we have the right to invite them or not invite them. To welcome them as guests is to proclaim that they are not really a part of the family. To welcome them as guests is to keep them separate and contained. To welcome them as guests is to state, although perhaps more nicely than we do many other times, that they are not related to us. If we really believe, however, that they, like all of us, are made in the image and likeness of God, then

crap

they are not our guests, and we are not their hosts. God is the host, and all of us are God's family, gathered around the dinner table. There are always people we are less comfortable with at large family gatherings. There are the people who don't dress properly, who don't use appropriate table manners, or who tell off-color jokes at family holidays. If they are family, however, we keep eating with them and celebrating together. We manage to put up with their flaws and faults, as they so graciously put up with ours.

The LGBTQIA+ community, and the trans* community in particular, may not always look like our "typical" churchgoers. They are more likely to have vividly colored hair and tattoos than the average Episcopalian or mainline churchgoer. They will definitely be more diverse than most Episcopal congregations along racial and ethnic lines. Some may be homeless. Others may be working in the sex trade, as unemployment is very high for trans* people. They are more likely to have been victims of violence than the average American, and more likely to be HIV positive. Their clothing styles may be quite different from the more traditional staid attire, or at least more casual. They may make some of us uncomfortable; they are not the traditional demographic most churches are trying to reach. In fact, their presence may scare some of our more traditional churchgoers. There may be women with oddly low voices, or men who are shorter than most men and do not have visible Adam's apples. Others, however, are indistinguishable from our general Sunday morning congregations. I suspect there are already a number of trans* people who are a part of our communities, but choose to live in stealth. Those who conform most closely to expected gender norms will probably be the easiest for congregations to accept. Stereotypes, however, are harmful, as there is no one model for what a trans* person is like, or how they will choose to present themselves. It is a widely diverse community, and that is a gift that they bring to our churches, which often are fairly homogeneous. Our role is not to decide if they fit in our congregation, but to accept them as members of the family of God, and hence as our siblings.

We can continue to exclude trans* people; after all, we could continue in pretty much the same way we have been operating for many years, and most trans* people will get the unspoken message: "you are not welcome in our places of worship." Our congregations might be a lot more comfortable, but we would be missing their gifts. We would miss the individual gifts that God has given each and every one of them. We would also miss the gift that God gave to the trans* community for our sake, for in their diversity, in their challenge to binary forms of gender, they call us to imagine God in ways that break us out of those binary boxes into which we have tried to stuff not only humankind, but God as well. They remind us that human beings, made in the image and likeness of a God who cannot be fully comprehended by human beings, are also complex, mysterious, and beyond our attempts to simplify them into easily managed categories. Most of all, trans* people challenge us to live up to Christ's admonition to love one another. As the author of the First Letter of John reminds us, "Beloved, let us love one another, because love is from God; everyone who loves is born of God and knows God. Whoever does not love does not know God, for God is love."[5] Christians have not always been loving to trans* people. Indeed, many parts of Christianity are still hostile to the whole LGBTQIA+ community, and to trans* people in particular. If we are to witness that we are the Church that follows Christ, we need to show that we love all, and not just those who make

---

[5] 1 John 4:7–8.

us comfortable. Acknowledging that trans* people are indeed made in God's image and likeness and that we are called to love them as we are called to love all of God's children is one of God's gifts in our time. May we learn to truly love one another, for love—all love—is from God, who is Love.

Epilogue: Through Fear to Hope

When my son sent us the e-mail telling us that he was trans*, my first emotion was fear. Not the simple fear of the unknown, or the fear that we were moving into difficult areas. Instead, it was that gut-clenching fear that comes when you are desperately afraid for yourself or for someone whom you love. It was the kind of fear that leaves you cold and feeling helpless. It is the kind of fear that almost paralyzes you. I was horribly afraid for my beloved child.

I had known other trans* people, and I had no problems with the idea that some people had gender identities that did not match the genders they were assigned at birth. I had studied gender and gender issues, and I understood the variety of ways that gender is experienced and expressed. From that base of knowledge, I absolutely believed two things. First, I believed that to live a life of authenticity, to be the person God had created him to be, my son would need to transition. He could not continue to live his life trying to be someone he was not. The second thing I believed, every bit as clearly, was that in transitioning, my son would open himself up to much more discrimination than he would have faced as a woman. In many states, such discrimination continues to be legal. He would also potentially be subject to more physical violence than he would have been as a cis-presenting woman. The knowledge of the way that trans* people are treated in our culture fueled my fear.

I had tried, as he grew up, to prepare him for a world that was, in many ways, still highly discriminatory of and violent toward women. I thought I had prepared my child for the fight that is still necessary for women who are trying to excel in areas that are not traditionally feminine. I thought I had taught him how to survive as a woman in a world where women are still valued less than men, where what they have to offer is often devalued or ignored. I took pride in his independence, his strength, and his refusal to be bound by traditional gender roles. I had done my best to prepare him to live as a woman.

When I read his e-mail, when I realized that I had been raising two sons and not a son and a daughter, when he told us he was trans*, I realized I had been preparing him for the wrong type of experience, and, most importantly, I had been preparing him for the wrong set of problems. I realized that I had little advice to offer him about how to navigate a world where many would argue that people like him do not even exist: they are confused, or mentally ill, or even possessed by Satan. I had not prepared him for a world where even many people who decry discrimination against most persecuted groups still argue for such practices against the trans* community. I realized that my efforts to try to protect him, at least somewhat, from the brokenness of our world were going to be much less effective than I had assumed. Like many women throughout the world who know deep down that they are powerless to keep their children safe, I felt grief and anger and fear. Since he was living away from home, in a different state, I could not protect him from those who saw, in his identification as trans*, the chance to sexually harass him without any repercussions. He was blessed that his good friends stood beside him and that there was a supportive community at his college. But he endured, as I learned later but feared from that first moment, stalking by a student whom the college would not discipline, and was passed over for an academic award he richly deserved.

A phrase often attributed to Tip O'Neill declares, "All politics is local," and that certainly was true for me. Although for a long time I had supported trans* rights and voted against those who practiced discrimination against anyone, advocating for basic civil rights for the trans* community became a passion. I joined groups on Facebook, I went to marches in support of trans* rights, and on the Trans* Day of Remembrance I attended services remembering those who had died. I wanted to immerse myself in the struggle as an ally, hoping that we were moving toward a world that would be kinder and more just for members of the trans* community. For a while, all that activity fed my hope. It seemed that we, as a country, were indeed moving in a positive direction. While there was still much to be done, it appeared the tide had turned.

It was during this time—as I kept saying someone should write a book on theology for trans* allies in order to counteract some of the really horrible theology I was encountering—that I first came to entertain the possibility that this book was my call. It took me a while to accept that call. I thought it ought to be a trans* voice that spoke, and I didn't want to presume to speak for the trans* community. The call to write also required me to step out of my specialty of spirituality and practical theology into constructive and even Trinitarian theology, areas that had not been high on my list in my doctoral studies. But I have found that if you ignore a call, God often speaks more clearly.

I have often heard the voice of God through the voices of other people. While attending a rally in Massachusetts to support keeping all public accommodations open to the trans* community, I talked with a trans* activist who told me that if I really wanted to be an ally, what I needed to do was talk to other cis people. So it was that I contacted an editor I knew at Church Publishing to see if there might be interest in this book. In a reasonably short time, my proposal was approved, and I began to do the necessary work to learn a new area of knowledge in order to try to make a real contribution. This was all still in that heady time of hope.

I should have recalled, from my study of other movements of social progress, that backlash almost always occurs after a time of progress. That certainly was the case with trans* rights. By the time I finished my research and was ready to begin writing, it was no longer the time of optimism in which I had first envisioned this proposal, but the latter part of the 2016 campaign, when hate speech was becoming acceptable public discourse, and violence was rising against the trans* community. They, like other persecuted communities, were being used to generate fear to sway voters.

I was no longer sure what to write, or how to write this book. The fear returned tenfold, and I began to worry about the danger that I was putting my family in by even attempting such a work. It was one thing to be willing to stand out in front in this time of hate and division in our country and risk the danger personally, but I was terrified by the thought I might be putting my family into danger by my witness. In spite of their encouragement to continue with what I was doing, I was, once again, paralyzed by fear.

I would love to tell you that I prayed about it and all my fear evaporated. I guess that happens to some people, but that is not the way God normally works in my life. Instead, God helped me to journey through the fear. Slowly, ever so slowly, the book started to take shape. Sometimes, it felt as if I were caught in quicksand. At other points, something would happen to ignite my fears into a hotter fire, and I would turn away from the heat. Each time, however, I eventually returned to the work, a work I could not ignore.

Although God never took away the fear, God was with me through that fear, helping me to find signs of hope in the midst of all that was going on around me. Most of the signs of hope were people I saw standing up against fear and hate. My Facebook groups showed me many dedicated allies and parents facing far more difficult things than I was facing, and courageously loving and supporting their children. The Presiding Bishop of the Episcopal Church and my own diocesan bishops publicly decried the rising anti-trans* sentiment. One of my trans* friends, who has been witnessing under difficult situations and changing minds in a part of the country that is notoriously homophobic and transphobic, has been an inspiration and a reminder that, as an ally, my role may be difficult, but it is not nearly as difficult as the role played by those within the trans* community. But most of all, I saw lots of pretty ordinary people standing up for the LGBT community, and the trans* community in particular, and I saw those advocating for various persecuted communities coming together to support each other. In that joining, I saw the Holy Spirit at work, and I was reminded that with God all things are possible. I was reminded that, no matter how difficult things get, Good Friday is never the end of the story.

I do not understand God's plan, but that is not surprising. For if God is beyond all that we can imagine, how can we expect to understand how God is working everything out? I am not quite sure how we will get from our broken world to God's reign. However, Jesus actually left pretty easy instructions for finding the right path. Knowing that humans can argue endlessly about who is right and who is wrong, Jesus gave his disciples only two rules. Love God with all your heart, and love your neighbor as yourself. When I am afraid, or when I am tempted to despair, I look for those whose love of God and love of other people reminds me that the nature of God is love. As a hymn in the Episcopal hymnal reminds us, "God is love, and where true love is, God himself is there."[1] Those words continue to help me to move through fear to hope. In the end, the love of God is the deep well of hope that never runs dry. One day, I pray that the world may truly know that we are Christians by our love.

---

[1] *The Hymnal 1982* (New York: The Church Hymnal Corp., 1985): #577.

Printed in the USA
CPSIA information can be obtained
at www.ICGtesting.com
LVHW021317091023
760577LV00009B/337

9 780898 690057